Doug

Dare to Dream

*From tragedy to triumph:
A daredevil's ride*

A Memoir as told to Steven R. Hall

Copyright © 2020 by Steven R. Hall and Douglas Senecal

All rights reserved. No part of this book may be reproduced or transmitted in any form or by any means, electronic or mechanical, including photocopying, recording, or by any information storage and retrieval system without permission in writing from the publisher.

ISBN 978-1-7343729-2-2

15 Rules Publishing

54 Old Farm Road

Sturbridge, MA 01566

www.15Rules.com

www.DougDanger.net

Cover photos courtesy of Chad Coppess

https://www.facebook.com/Dakotagraph/

Table Of Contents

Acknowledgments 1

Prologue 8

Chapter 1: The Family Waits.........................12

Chapter 2: A Kid Dreams Big 26

Chapter 3: A Dream Is Born...........................49

Chapter 4: From The Minors To The Majors.60

Chapter 5: Reaching For The Stars.................79

Chapter 6: It's Getting Serious Now 107

Chapter 7: The Long Road Back 112

Chapter 8: Confidence Turns To Calamity ..129

Chapter 9: Death Is No Match For Me........135

Chapter 10: A Tale Of Two Legends 147

Chapter 11: Riding Into The Sunset 183

Chapter 12: Doubt, Fear, And Other Demons 193

Chapter 13: Casting A Shadow 202

About The Author...211

References...212

Acknowledgments

In my nearly six decades on this earth and forty-plus years of performing as Doug Danger, I have been blessed with many caring family members, friends, and fans. I owe a debt of gratitude to you for your kindness, generosity, and love. Without your support, my life and story would undoubtedly be different.

Mom, you've been my rock and my biggest supporter, encourager, and fan. You are the reason I am who I am. You are the best, Mom. I love you dearly.

To my late stepfather Arthur, who was there for me and treated me as one of his own, I am genuinely grateful to have had you in my life.

To my late father, thank you for always listening and telling me to go after my dreams. It meant the world to me.

To my brother Mike and his wife Tammi, I am grateful for you in my life. Mike, when the chips were down, you made me come out a winner. I always knew you were only a phone call away. Thanks for getting me to the other side so many times. You are the definition of an awesome big brother.

To my brother Tracy, thank you for your encouragement and your sometimes tough love. Without you and Mike in my life, I would not be the man I am today.

To Tina, the mother of my two children, I thank you kindly for your continued friendship and for giving me two of the most wonderful children a man could have.

Maria, my wife, you make me whole. I thank God every day for putting you in my life. I went from the bottom of the ladder to the top. Then I crashed and fell back to the bottom. Thanks for turning my life around. We made it back to the top!

To my daughter Holly, as a young and beautiful little girl you taught me the true meaning of love. When I was dealing with my head injury, and when I was discouraged, struggling, and suffering emotional pain, you gave my life meaning. To this day, I cherish the moments when you would run to me screaming, "Daddy's home! Daddy's home!" when I walked in the door. With your hands in the air, you'd jump into my arms. Your warm, affectionate hug and your beautiful, loving smile were rays of sunshine that kept me going when the rest of the world seemed unsure how to help me.

To my son Scott, I am so proud of the strong man you have become. You may not realize this, but as you were growing up, on those days when I was there for you, you were also there for me. Being your father gave my life meaning and helped me through my struggles. Working together, we made it. I love you dearly.

Lou, you have been a best friend for decades, and I am so grateful for your friendship. Thanks for being part of my dream and helping me make it come true.

Steve, Janet, and Craig, you are the best of friends. Thanks for making another dream come true with this book.

A very special thanks to my dear friend, Lathan McKay. I cannot say enough. You gave me the opportunity to rewrite the history books. Thank you from the bottom of my heart. And from all of the Evel Knievel fans in the world, I extend another thank you for opening up the Evel

Knievel Museum in Topeka, Kansas. You are so unique in the greatest of ways.

Robbie Hull, thank you so much for your amazing art on my helmets.

Mike Patterson, thank you for welcoming us into Historic Harley-Davidson and having Dave Larson prepare Evel's bike for the jumps.

Woody, Marilyn, and Manny, thank you for hosting one of the greatest jumps in history and for making it a world-class affair at the incomparable Buffalo Chip Campground in Sturgis, South Dakota.

I'd like to thank the following people for helping me fulfill my dreams: Gaspare and Anne Re, Biz and Charlotte, Uncle Ronnie, Tommy Skura, Roger Durkee, Phil Dube, Ed Roy, Mark and Pete Pessolano, Richard and Barry Lundgren, Mike and Maria Wade, Mike and the entire crew at Vanson Leathers, Jay at Spectro Oil, Bell Helmets, Pathfinder's High School Carpentry, Machine Shop, and Blueprinting Departments.

Arlene Shea, Dr. Conner, Dr. Wexler, Dr. Siddiqui, Dr. Lowen, and Anise, thank you for saving my life!

Melody, thanks for helping me believe in myself after my crash.

Russ Conway, Paul Cote and Sue, Jack Brady, Tim and Joie Chitwood, Tonny Peterson, Jake Plumstead, Dwayne Verron, Gary Schoonover, Julius Rosa, "Wrongway" (Justin Bellinger), Jeff Bursey, Laurieanne, Jim "Crash" Moreau, Kenny Galyas, Chuck Fortsen, Nate Olsen, George Sedlack (Evel's painter), Mike Draper, and Dennis Tomczak and Gene Payne (Harley-Davidson mechanics in Sturgis)—Thank you all for working with me on numerous successful performances.

Doug Klang, thanks for being incredible on the microphone; Chad Coppess, thank you for recording my life; Dennis McCurdy, thank you for your inspiring words when I needed them; and Margo Chevers, you are enormously missed.

Thank you, Rita Schiano, Charlie Cook, Robbie Knievel, Kelly Knievel, Debbie Lawler, Travis Pastrana, Seth Enslow, Todd Seeley, Debbie Trent, Father Swift, and Ryan Cavanaugh for inspiring me.

Mark Pluta, thank you for building my world record bike and being a true friend when I really needed one.

Thanks to all my friends at the Quaboag Riders Motorcycle Club.

A special thanks to Aleda and Neil from Raceway Ambulance.

Thanks, Kenny G., Billy T-Cats, Dean Sasen, Derrick and Anne, and JC and Richard for all the selfless help throughout the years.

Thank you to the Palmer and Monson Police Departments for a few breaks in life—with a lesson.

Thank you, Turley Publications, for the coverage through the years. Thank you, Kitty, for lying with me through months of chemotherapy.

Evel Knievel, thank you for being a friend, inspiring our country, creating a dream for me, and allowing me to believe I could make it come true.

Thank you to the many more friends and fans who have stepped up to help and/or given me words of encouragement. You mean the world to me.

Finally, God, thank you for being my friend, and thank you for everything. I learned there is no such thing as a coincidence. I've lived through things I never should have, and I've seen miracles before my eyes. Is it really that difficult to believe in a higher power? Talk to God and find peace.

Sincerely,

Doug Danger

Prologue

"Life's greatest challenges can become life's greatest successes."
~ Doug Danger ~

Do you have goals, dreams, and desires that you keep locked inside?

Why do we hold back?

We hold back because of discouragement and two overrated emotions: doubt and fear. We doubt our abilities, and we fear failure, success, pain (emotional and physical), and the unknown. Doubts and fears prevent you from flourishing. Doubts and fears probably paint a far worse picture in your head than reality actually is.

In the profound words of President Theodore Roosevelt, "It is not the critic who counts; not the man who points out how the strong man stumbles ... The credit belongs to the man in the arena, whose face is marred by dust and sweat and blood; who strives valiantly; who errs, who comes short again and again because there is no effort without error and shortcoming ... who at ... best knows ... the triumph of high achievement, and who at the worst, if he fails, at least fails while daring greatly, so that his place shall never be with those cold and timid souls who neither know victory nor defeat."

Cold and timid souls live with doubt and fear. Cold and timid souls have unfulfilled dreams and desires, and their lives are not well lived.

You are far more capable than you or others may think. You are far more capable than you can imagine! Greatness isn't something you are born with; it's taught, it's learned, and it's practiced. Breaking away from doubt and fear is the key to reaching your highest potential and true happiness.

You have been given this gift: your one and only life. You are cheating your creator, yourself, your loved ones, and society if you don't achieve all you are capable of and all you desire. You deserve no less.

In preparing this book, I've learned more about overcoming doubt and fear and achieving all you desire by getting incredible insight into the mind of the man known to the world as Doug Danger. Moreover, although I've known Doug since early childhood (over 50 years), this endeavor has allowed me to see even deeper into the soul of my cousin and friend, who I knew as Doug Senecal while we were growing up.

I now more profoundly appreciate my friendship with this motivational speaker, who is also, quite possibly, one of the most insightful, skillful, and capable stunt performers of our lifetime. Despite his talent, fame, and notoriety, Doug Danger remains humble, warm, and generous with his time.

In this memoir, we delve into the mind of a man who from a very young age, dared to dream of achieving heights that once seemed impossible. A visionary who chose motorcycle stunts as his craft, he demonstrated that with courage, strength, and determination, "impossibilities" ARE achievable—even when he was faced with overwhelming life challenges and near-death experiences that took him far beyond the public world of entertainment and daredevilry.

From early adversity and humble beginnings, Doug's journey has taken him through an array of highs and lows. These include recognition in the *Guinness Book of World Records* after leaping 251 feet over an astounding 42 cars in 1991, a devastating head injury, overcoming stage four cancer, and completing a leap at the age of 53 across 22 cars on Evel Knievel's authentic 1972 Harley-Davidson XR750. Doug continues to defy the odds in a spectacular way, while simultaneously working to succeed in business, love, and friendship.

As we review his remarkable story more closely, I hope you will begin to understand, as I do, that defying these odds went far beyond good fortune. I'd argue that once you get to know Doug Danger, you will see that success over adversity takes courage, hard work, determination, strength, perseverance, a positive mental attitude, intelligent thought, a good team around you, and yes, a lot of dumb luck.

So, grab ahold of those bars, twist that throttle, and squeeze the tank with your knees, because we're going for a ride into the Danger Zone.

Chapter 1
The Family Waits

"I'm not afraid of death; death's afraid of me."
~ Doug Danger ~

Much like she had during the 28 unimaginably painful days before, Doug's exhausted wife, Tina, sat once again next to her young husband, grieving, waiting, and longing for any improvement. Yet there he lay, still battered and bruised from the devastating 70 mile-per-hour motorcycle crash head-on into a solid cement wall. She watched this man, still motionless, withering away in that cold, stark, and sterile intensive care unit, with the only evidence of life being the heart monitor's incessant beeping and the squiggly lines on the screen. From him there came not a blink, not a twitch, not a moan.

Would he ever wake from the coma? She prayed for strength and a miracle, even though she had been warned by the medical team that she should just treasure the time they had together. If he were to unexpectedly pull through, they said, with the extent of his brain injuries he undoubtedly would not be the man she once knew and loved.

As she looked over all the needles, tubes, and apparatuses keeping his motionless body alive, she wondered if she had made the right decision, in the beginning, to keep him on life support.

It was not supposed to be like this, she thought. After all, he had just received the big break he'd been waiting for: a contract guaranteeing $250,000, plus a percentage of the pay-per-view telecast receipts. This disastrous crash happened during what was supposed to be the last of three jumps before that scheduled pay-per-view event: a televised "jump-off" against Robbie Knievel, the son of the world-renowned legend Evel Knievel, and a legend in his own right. These were "small" jumps (10-11 cars), he had assured her; there was no reason to be worried. It was true; he had accomplished hundreds, maybe thousands, of these jumps before in practice and public performances throughout North America. After all, it's essential to keep busy performing, he'd said, to avoid getting nervous when attempting the big jumps. The possibility of a tragedy like this current situation had never crossed her mind. Moreover, he was Doug Danger. He had never made a significant mistake before.

It's No Big Deal

It was a routine jump (if motorcycle jumping ever becomes routine) that Sunday in early June. The jump was held at a racetrack where he had appeared several times before over his career: Hudson Speedway in Hudson, New Hampshire. That day, as per usual at these small stock car racetracks, the event involved a quick setup of the ramps, some wheelies, then an 11-car jump as part of the halftime activities, followed by a quick teardown. Doug expressed some concern regarding the higher wind speeds that day. However, as he did many times before, he planned to compensate for the wind speed and direction by aiming his 500cc motorcycle slightly to the left side of the takeoff ramp, since the wind was coming in at his left side. He'd watch for higher wind gusts by observing the large American flag on his approach, and offset accordingly. If need be, he could slow the speed just a little to compensate for a wind gust coming in from behind him.

With most of the crowd on their feet, cheering loudly on this sunny, warm, late June day in 1992, Doug Danger rounded the fourth turn and glanced at the flag, which, as he'd feared, was fluttering wildly at a 45-degree angle to his left and back side. Doug was a man of his word; he was not going to back off. He peered down at his speedometer and rolled ever so slightly off the throttle to compensate for the wind gust as he hit the large metal takeoff ramp and courageously launched into the air.

Maybe he had grown too confident in his ability; maybe he should have called off that approach and circled the track one more time; or perhaps he simply misjudged the strength of that gust, but as soon as Doug hit the apex of his flight, the tragedy began to unfold. The back end of his Honda started to drift to the right. For those in the motorcycle world, this is better known as a cross-up. And it was a nasty cross-up. Even worse, the fierce wind resulted in the motorcycle flying much farther than expected as the motorcycle's front-end rose considerably too high.

Long before touchdown, near the bottom of the landing ramp, it certainly appeared that Doug made corrections to his flight. Review of the video shows he tapped the rear brake to correct the front end, which was rising too high; he also tweaked the handlebars to the right to aim the bike parallel to the direction of travel, but the impact was just too great for him to maintain control.

In one horrifying instant, Doug's left hand was ripped off the handlebars and he was uncontrollably tossed onto, but not over, the bike's handlebars, dangling and dancing atop the out-of-control motorcycle while his right hand twisted the throttle even further to the wide-open position. Instead of turning sharp left to go around the oval track, the bike careened to the right, straight into the first turn's solid cement wall. In a cloud of dust, and over the horrified screams of onlookers, the front wheel impacted the wall a nanosecond before Doug's head, and then his body made impact at full speed. The bike broke into pieces, his helmet split, and he was tossed violently back from the direction he had just traveled. His body landed, lifeless and unimaginably twisted, on the track's unyielding pavement.

How could he have survived? Some mothers and fathers grabbed their children to hold them closer and comfort them; some left their seats to spare themselves and their children any more of the gruesome spectacle.

The ambulance crew, seemingly unprepared for such acute trauma, was slow to respond. When they finally arrived at the scene, it became very apparent that they were not EMTs and that they were poorly equipped. The ambulance attendants quickly realized they didn't even have a working bottle of oxygen.

No one remembers how this lack of oxygen and their unpreparedness was communicated to the crowd. Still, within just a few minutes, a quick-thinking trauma center nurse and spectator named Arlene Shea approached the track's protective fencing with a full bottle of oxygen. When she tried to hand it to the ambulance workers through the fence, she couldn't get their attention. So she ran to the pit entrance adjacent to the grandstands to get on the track. When she arrived there, the gate attendant wouldn't let her in, stating that she didn't have a pit pass. She pointed to where Doug was lying and said to the attendant, "That man on the track is hurt, and he needs me badly." When the attendant looked to where she was pointing, she hurriedly shoved him, causing him to stumble backward and fall over a nearby guardrail. Without hesitation, she darted past the guard and onto the racetrack, running for her life to save another.

When she arrived on the scene, she took a pulse but found none. She listened for breathing, but heard none. She wondered how long it had taken her to get to her car, get the oxygen, and get back down on the track. How long had his heart been stopped? How long had he not been breathing? In other words, how long had Doug Danger been clinically dead? Arlene worried that she would not be able to save this incredible daredevil.

She shouted out instructions to the ambulance attendants. "Hold this oxygen bag on him and squeeze it every five seconds to get oxygen in him!" She then initiated CPR before untangling his broken arm and leg and proceeding to splint them. They transferred him carefully but hurriedly to a backboard and into the ambulance.

The ambulance driver took it upon himself to bypass the two closest hospitals and race as fast as possible on the two-lane New Hampshire back roads to the St. Joseph Hospital trauma center in Nashua, a decision that was later deemed to be a determining factor that saved his life.

Along the way, Arlene and the ambulance team continued CPR until finally, with tears of joy in her eyes, an exhausted Arlene announced that she felt a pulse. The ambulance crew and Arlene estimate that it had been an astonishing 30 minutes since his heart stopped pumping on its own.

The ER trauma team at St. Joseph Hospital had been alerted about the severity of Doug's injuries and was awaiting his arrival. They systematically began to treat the most pressing of his injuries, which included a severe head injury, bilateral pneumothorax, a fractured skull, and several broken bones.

Thank God the top trauma specialist was present that day. Dr. Conner is a board-certified physician with over 30 years of experience, and using the knowledge he had gained over those years, he began to piece Doug back together.

Doug underwent surgery. His lungs were re-inflated with the use of a chest tube, and several of his bones (femur, tibia, clavicle, and wrists) had to be stabilized with metal rods, plates, and screws and supported with fiberglass casts. After surgery, his team of physicians closely monitored him while he was in the ICU. Labs and diagnostics revealed that his organs were beginning to fail. When that happened, Dr. Conner decided to put Doug on life support. And then the waiting game began.

The hospital contacted Doug's close family members and notified them about the accident and the gravity of his injuries. Family members put jobs and lives on hold to be by his side and help in any way they could, many traveling hundreds of miles to reach him as quickly as possible.

On a flight from Florida to get to the hospital, Doug's mother Marge and his brother Mike received word about the extent of Doug's injuries in a shocking way. Marge pulled out a *USA Today* newspaper from the pocket of the seat in front of her just to take her mind off of her worries and give her something to pass the time. When she opened to the sports section, the headline read, "Motorcycle Daredevil, Doug Danger, Hits Wall at Hudson Speedway, On Life

Support, Not Expected to Live." She almost threw up. Now her concern was whether she would make it in time to even say goodbye.

Mike and Marge arrived at Boston's Logan Airport and started the long trek to Nashua, New Hampshire. Marge remembers that the drive seemed like it would never end.

Doug's wife, Tina, was at the hospital with their six month-old daughter Holly, and greeted Mike and Marge when they arrived. She explained that Doug's condition was still critical and that the hospital would only allow one person at a time into the room, for five-minute increments.

Mike went in to see Doug first. When he came out, his face said it all. He trembled from head to toe and slowly shook his head from side to side as he wiped tears from his cheeks. The reality that he may have to say goodbye to his little brother was beginning to sink in.

Marge was then allowed to enter. She, too, shook visibly, but she staunchly squared her shoulders, knowing that she had to be there for her youngest son. Marge took a few moments to gain her strength before pushing open the room's heavy, cold steel door.

When she entered the room, Marge said she felt like she had walked into a bad horror film. One of Doug's eyes, though lifeless, was open and swelled to three times the size of the other. Steel rods stuck out of his broken nose. Airbags held his leg together. The respirator made a loud mechanical "breathing" noise as it inflated the lungs in her son's battered body. Shocked, Marge took in the scene, then turned and headed out of the room. She had barely made it through the door when her knees buckled and she lost consciousness, passing out from the horrible sight of her youngest son's fight for life. Nurses rushed to revive her and then helped her into a chair to recuperate. She couldn't go back in there; it was just too much.

Two days later, a nurse came to talk to Marge, Mike, and Tina. She told them that Doug continued to show brain activity even though he was unable to rouse and respond. She said it was imperative for him to hear the voices of those closest to him—especially his mother.

After that conversation, Marge became determined to assist her son out of his coma. She entered the room, cringing at the sight before her, but pressed on and took a seat by Doug's bed. She took his hand in hers and whispered into his ear, "I love you, Doug. I need you to get better so we can sit and laugh at all the stupid stuff nobody else ever gets. Please don't give up. We're here for you."

With the pain only a mother could know, she wiped tears from her eyes and left the room, having lost the strength to conceal her grief or hold her composure any longer. Mike and Tina took their turns talking to Doug and left the room in the same solemn condition as Marge.

Two weeks into Doug's coma, Dr. Conner met with the family and explained that Doug couldn't remain on the respirator any longer without having more permanent procedures done (i.e., a tracheostomy). Additionally, artificial ventilation causes an elevated risk of respiratory and multisystem failure. After a family meeting to discuss and weigh the options, the family members huddled together, said a prayer, and gave Dr. Conner consent to proceed with Doug's Advanced Directives and with the developed plan of care.

Those who gathered in that waiting room were worried; this was the day they secretly feared, but they did not want to voice those fears aloud. Would this be the day they lost a husband, son, brother, and father? Dr. Connor left the room to put the plan of care into motion.

Fortunately, the wait was not long. Within 20 minutes, Dr. Conner returned with the good news: Doug was successfully extubated and breathing on his own. At his fateful words, the group let out a huge sigh of relief.

Back to Reality

Now, almost a month after the accident, a stressed and exhausted Tina was sitting at Doug's bedside once more. She'd been managing all the responsibilities thrown into her lap and experiencing long days of travelling back and forth from Palmer MA, to Nashua NH, while still working a full-time job and taking care of their 6 month-old daughter. Little did she know, however, that this day would soon be different than the previous 28 days.

First, miraculously, she saw her husband's left index finger twitch. She gasped, and her heart beat a little faster. Had she genuinely seen that, or was her mind playing tricks on her? She studied her husband's lifeless body for another sign. Perhaps this was the hint of hope she had longed for.

Nothing happened for several long minutes, but then she saw another twitch of the same finger, followed by a slight movement in two more digits of his same hand. Her heart began to race.

Tina gently caressed the back of Doug's hand for just a moment, careful not to disrupt the plastic tube and the needle that pierced his skin. Then she stood up, glanced at him lovingly, and excitedly darted out to the nurse's station to alert them of the good news.

Chapter 2
A Kid Dreams Big

"Life is not lived by the timid, but by the dreamer."
~ Doug Danger ~

By the time 5 year-old Doug and his father arrived in Dad's battered, sun-faded gray Chevy step-side pickup, there wasn't a place to park within a mile of the iconic site located on the famous Las Vegas Strip. So, Bob Senecal pulled into the first open spot he could find, and the two began their trek to the now historic venue. At that moment, each recognized that this show was going to be unlike anything seen in this city before.

In the distance, the distinctive fountains of Caesar's Palace came into view, and the rumble of the crowd grew noticeably louder with each footstep. Throngs of police cars and motorcycles with their flashing lights on created an overstimulated atmosphere in this already flashy city.

As Doug and his dad got closer to the venue, they recognized why the event merited so much attention from the Las Vegas police department. The masses gathered to see this spectacle were shoulder-to-shoulder, nearly spilling out into the traffic-filled street. Police officers barked out orders to corral the enthusiastic patrons into the already overcrowded casino grounds.

You could feel the excitement in the air as the massive crowd waited in eager anticipation for the event to begin. People from all walks of life had gathered: young and old, well-dressed businessmen and women, costumed casino workers, and tourists in shorts with cameras around their necks. Even the locals, who appeared unfazed by the circus-like atmosphere, were there. All of them were chattering up a storm and squeezing as close as they could to get a better view. They had come to witness a young, unknown man with the crazy name of Evel Knievel attempt to jump his motorcycle over the casino's fountains.

For young Doug, now perched on his father's shoulders, the scene in his hometown was chaotic and a bit overwhelming. His dad strategically worked his way around and through the huge crowd to try to get a better view for himself and his son.

From Doug's vantage point atop his father's shoulders and a dozen rows back, he eyed the reason they had come: three iconic water fountains with two large wooden ramps on each side. He marveled at the space between them. Even at that young age, Doug appreciated the distance the daredevil would have to fly.

Before long he was able to get a glimpse of a man, riding on a beautifully loud masterpiece of a motorcycle—a 500cc Triumph T100—as he roared into the arena through a narrow parting of the masses.

Doug Danger recalled, "It was probably the first major event I remember attending as a child. He [Knievel] was wearing a nearly all-white leather racing suit with a couple of red and blue stripes. People were everywhere, loud as hell, but when he started talking on the mic, they quieted down to listen. I was blown away by the attention this one man could attract. He had that way about him."

In reality, the casino must not have expected such an enormous crowd to attend, because the performer only had a single microphone tied into a small amplifying system to address the crowd. Like most, Doug was unable to hear his address. Those who did hear it, however, said it was a masterful speech, as always.

Doug Danger vividly recalled, "Damn, I was there with my dad at Evel's Caesar's Palace jump." It was New Year's Eve, 1967.

That fateful day created a legend. Nearly everybody knows that Evel Knievel became one of the most iconic and masterful showmen of the 20th century and is basically the father of extreme sports. Most people also know that Evel Knievel's leap over the center fountain was spectacularly unsuccessful in the most violent way.

On the far side of the fountains, with the front wheel raised so high that it nearly flipped him over backward, Evel Knievel crash-landed that 400-pound motorcycle short of the landing ramp onto a piece of plywood laid haphazardly on the roof of a cargo van parked up against the landing ramp.

The impact onto that roof was so brutal that it immediately catapulted Evel over the handlebars, tossed him and his motorcycle to the ground, and threw him around like a ragdoll in the teeth of an angry junkyard dog.

Smoke rose from the chaos, carnage, and clanging of the motorcycle scraping on the pavement. However, the noise could barely be heard over the deafening screams of the shocked onlookers. Man and machine uncontrollably tumbled for what seemed to be an eternity before eventually coming to rest, both badly mangled, on the far side of the fountains, well beyond the landing ramp.

"You'd better get that kid outta' here. This ain't nothin' for a kid to see," scolded an unkempt, crotchety middle-aged woman balancing a non-filtered cigarette on her dry, nicotine-stained lips. Not fazed, Doug and his father turned from her glare to survey the gruesome scene that had just unraveled before their eyes.

"That started it all," Doug Danger stated with a chuckle. "With all due respect to my friend Evel Knievel, as a naive young boy who had not yet even ridden a bicycle, I thought to myself, 'Hey, I bet I could'a made that.'"

That moment did, in fact, start it all. Evel Knievel recovered and his career skyrocketed from there. As for little Doug Senecal, that spark ignited a flame. He discovered his future career that day—a career that eventually led him to be known to the world as perhaps the greatest motorcycle jumper of all time: Doug Danger.

It Don't Come Easy

Before we continue, it's important to note that those who have seen Doug Danger perform over the years have had the pleasure of witnessing a man who is one of the all-time masters at two-wheeled performances. It's awe-inspiring to see him demonstrate the sitting-on-the-seat wheelie. He is capable of performing these at incredibly high speeds, or even more difficult, at low speeds, stopping and starting at will. Moreover, he can hit targets or avoid obstacles with pinpoint accuracy, while never letting the front wheel touch the ground.

Just as impressive, he's well known for doing the same thing at blistering speeds while standing on the seat and precariously balancing on one foot. This feat takes incredible skill and balance and is rarely seen even in today's world of extreme sports.

More incredibly, he's been performing these skills masterfully (and seemingly easily) for over 40 years and counting. Of course, he also has the remarkable ability to do a two-wheeled dance while racing. But he's most famous for leaping incredible distances on modern-day motocross machines or on a $350,000 authentic museum piece: the 1972 Harley-Davidson XR750 once jumped by Evel Knievel himself. When not flying in the capable hands of the ageless Doug Danger, this famous bike is proudly on display at the Evel Knievel Museum adjacent to Historic Harley-Davidson in Topeka, Kansas (Museum, 2017).

With all that said, one would think that riding and balancing on any two-wheeled cycle must have come easily to Doug. But, perhaps as a small inspiration to us all, Doug explained that he in fact had a tough time learning to balance and ride on a bicycle, which he attempted just days after the Caesar's Palace jump inspired him.

"To a 5 year-old, our driveway was steep," Doug explained. "My father sat me on a huge bicycle, and after very little instruction, gave me a nudge down the hill. It was sort of like teaching a kid to swim by throwing him into a swimming pool without actually giving him meaningful instruction. Well, I drowned," he said with his usual jovial chuckle. "I crashed hard at the end of the driveway and got pretty skinned up!" It took him a couple of weeks before the scabs healed and he was ready to try again. "But this time I wised up and had [my older brother] Mike teach me."

He learned that day what a gift it is to have an older brother, and Mike has never let him down. Anytime Doug got himself in trouble, Mike showed up and made sure his little brother was safe.

Recently, Doug returned to Las Vegas and took a ride by the old family house to show his bride that "gigantic" hill. As it turns out (and as you might have guessed), it was just a small incline—about a 3-foot drop over a 30-foot long driveway.

It just goes to show: obstacles that once appeared daunting often seem trivial after you overcome them or put them in perspective.

Leaving Las Vegas

I first met Doug in the summer of 1968 when we were both 6 years old. I was playing in the yard at my grandparents' home when a wood-paneled station wagon pulled into the driveway. Suitcases were strapped to the roof rack and boxes were stacked in the very back of that large car.

I looked over in curiosity to see a flashy woman in her mid-30s with bright red hair, oversized sunglasses, and an infectious smile exit the wagon. Closely behind her followed a 6 year-old, wide-eyed, grinning kid who curiously turned his head every which way to survey this rural, wooded neighborhood of Palmer, Massachusetts. He was skinny as a rail, had long blond hair to his shoulders, and wore a collared t-shirt, tight jeans, and Converse-type sneakers (which weren't cool then, like they are now).

What I recall most is that even at his young age he had a confidence like few others. It didn't come across as arrogance or a brash attitude, but as innocent confidence and curiosity, as if he didn't understand how to be anything else. In other words, he always seemed to have a command of himself and his surroundings.

Yet despite this self-assurance, he was a young boy caught in family turmoil. His parents had made an abrupt split, which eventually resulted in the two of them divorcing.

With not much more than the clothes they had on their backs and a few suitcases, Marge ventured with Doug, Mike, and her mother-in-law back to her parents' home in Massachusetts to start a new life.

The circumstances were humbling and drastic for such a young boy, and the change certainly wasn't going to be easy.

In less than six months from that fateful day at Caesar's Palace, Doug's life and his relationship with his father had turned upside-down. He and his dad were now nearly 3,000 miles apart. As a child, he saw his father very infrequently after that. His father would pop in unexpectedly and usually only stay for minutes at a time. Although he tried to keep the hurt bottled up inside, it was evident to many who knew Doug that this experience was exceedingly difficult for him.

Times were tough for the Senecals in 1968 and the years to follow, especially without significant financial help from the boys' father. Marge took a labor position in a local egg carton factory, and Doug and his brother worked odd jobs until they were old enough to earn a paycheck legally. Doug had a newspaper route and traveled several miles every day on his bicycle in both the dead cold of winter and the heat of Massachusetts midsummers to deliver the evening edition.

It took well over a year, but the struggling family trio was finally able to afford to move into a small mobile home they parked in the backyard of Marge's parents' home. The trailer was the type with one bedroom in the back and a kitchen table that also served as a bed at night. They plugged their trailer into the electrical service of Marge's parents' home. This mobile home was to be their cramped accommodations for several more years.

One can imagine that these experiences hardened Doug. But in retrospect, they also made him more dependent on himself, and perhaps, gave him more confidence. This confidence gave rise to him being more of an independent thinker. That is, anything he desired he had to make happen himself.

For example, the teen boys in the neighborhood were passionate about both street and ice hockey. Every year, as the cool days of autumn turned to the chill of winter, neighborhood kids young and old, short and tall, would turn their attention from slamming and bashing each other for a chance to get the plastic street-hockey ball, to battling over a hockey puck (or a small wooden block carved to resemble a puck) on nearby Lake Thompson when it finally froze over. Moreover, as the playing surface turned from dirt to solid ice, the speed of the game ratcheted up tremendously.

Doug was a scrawny kid, a pre-teen beanpole, but he could scrap it out with the toughest, meanest, and biggest high school teens on the block! Of course, to participate you had to be tough. The boys didn't tolerate softies, and certainly the sight of blood (yours or someone else's) wasn't allowed to scare you. And believe me, there was plenty of blood to go around every time these wanna-be NHL bruisers got together. The higher speeds, combined with razor-sharp steel hockey blades and kids with more "balls" than talent, resulted in even more spilled blood and broken bones than one would imagine. The carnage was proportionate to the speed of the game, or at least it seemed that way.

Nonetheless, there was still no shortage of eager participants. Doug said that with so many kids wanting to join in, playing time was an issue—especially for a small, young kid like him—unless, however, you played goalie!

Goalies were hard to find. If one was fool enough to volunteer, he was hard to keep "healthy" among the barrage of big, bruising hockey wannabe's who could skate really fast but not stop so well, and who also had a bad habit of slamming into the goalie.

Now, if that goalie had real goalie equipment, things might not have been so bad. But only rich kids had actual hockey equipment, and there were no rich kids in this working-class neighborhood.

So, not wanting to miss out on playing time, Doug fashioned makeshift goalie padding using cardboard boxes and foam from an old mattress for arm and leg pads. He used a baseball glove for a mitt, and wore a baseball catcher's chest protector and mask. He was ready, or at least he thought he was.

"It looked stupid, but worked well; at least until it got wet," he recalled with a chuckle. "But I forgot something extremely important. The cup! I only had to get nailed once to start begging my Mom to take me to the sporting goods store to get one."

That was Doug, though. No excuses! If his family couldn't afford something, he'd fashion it. If someone needed him for a tough assignment, he would "take one for the team" and do it with his trademark, ear-to-ear smile.

No Circus Needed

On one occasion, I recall Doug coming home with a unicycle he picked up at a yard sale. Of course, it's not very often you see a unicycle at a yard sale, but somehow he found one. With no outside help or instruction (and without YouTube in the '70s for the play-by-play demonstration), day after day, for hours at a time, Doug methodically practiced until he mastered the unicycle. It was a sight to see: that boney, wide-eyed kid, grinning his show-all-the-teeth smile, hands outstretched to the side and concentrating to keep his balance, pedaling that one-wheeled contraption like an over-enthusiastic circus clown around his home and the neighborhood streets. He took great pride in the praise he'd get from passing cars or neighbors on their porches cheering him on.

In the same spirit and with the same dedication, at an early age he mastered juggling. He could juggle tennis balls or anything else that was available. And, yes, although he never ran away to join the circus, he would occasionally combine the two tricks, which I must say he did pretty well!

Then one day, seemingly satisfied with mastering these marvelous accomplishments, he just dropped them from his childhood repertoire. To this day, he says he still could ride a unicycle if he wanted to, and I've seen him juggle, but I haven't seen him combine the two in quite some time.

A Menace to Society

From childhood to now, Doug holds the men and women in blue, our brave police officers, in high regard. However, early on we were not sure that feeling was reciprocal.

By the time Doug was 13, his mother had remarried and they had moved to a home of their own in that same town, not far from the trailer in the grandparents' backyard. Doug's family had grown by one with the addition of a new stepbrother, Tracy, who is about six months older than Doug.

Doug's new stepfather, Arthur, was a good man, but one of those old-time men who did not have a "warm and fuzzy" exterior. He was gruff, to put it lightly. As kids, it was always wise for us to walk on eggshells when he was nearby. But deep down, he was protective of his new family—including Doug.

Doug "Danger" Senecal 1975

Long before we were old enough to drive, Doug and I would get together by bicycling the five miles to each other's homes. One particular afternoon, I rolled into their downtown Palmer home just in time to witness a Palmer Police officer knocking at the front door. However, that was not an unusual sight to see. Policemen stopping by had become a regular occurrence. Doug was well known down at the station for his antics with the unicycle, riding wheelies down

Main Street, skateboarding anywhere he shouldn't have been, and building and racing wooden soapbox type cars down local (rather large) hills while dodging annoyed drivers and homeowners. He often trampled the latter's beautiful flowers when he or a friend would wreck. We laughed about those crashes hysterically... until the green-thumbed homeowner found out, that is. We can say that we learned a little about landscaping in those days, having to replant and rake what we tore up.

As I crept around the corner of the house to try to get an inkling about the reason for the visit by Palmer's finest this time, Arthur opened the door. Annoyed by yet another police visit, in his usual gruff way he barked loudly at the police officer, "What the hell do you want now?" Yes, that is how often they were at the house, and yes, that's almost as close as I recall Arthur ever showing "love" for his stepson, but he did.

Doug was never involved in anything that might be considered hurtful or harmful to others. Well, unless you count the time he set up precariously balanced ramps on the town sidewalks and jumped his bike over naïve but enthusiastic neighborhood kids. But he certainly had a knack for causing a lot of police officers to shake their heads at him.

During his early childhood, bicycle wheelies down crowded Main Street seemed to draw their attention. I recall one incident when Doug and I were bicycling down a neighboring town's Main Street, and I heard the short blip of a police cruiser's siren behind us. Surprised, I turned to see Doug precariously balancing one of his trademark wheelies. With serious and total concentration, he carefully worked the pedals. He'd turn them fast, slow, or pause them as needed while he turned the handlebars and twisted his body every which way to keep the bike steered in the right direction. He remained up on one wheel, inches from the sidewalk or around the numerous parked cars, all the while ignoring the police vehicle behind him. The cruiser's lights continued flashing, and it carried an obviously irritated police officer. After a short time, Doug rounded onto a side street, dropped the front wheel, and stopped for the officer.

"Why didn't you stop for me back there?" the annoyed officer called out as he approached the two of us.

"I was going for a new personal record and was almost there," Doug quickly replied with a big grin. "That telephone pole right there is number eight! A new record: eight telephone poles!"

He got off with another warning and the usual shake of the officer's head.

Always a Performer

Some might think that Doug's motivation is the thrill of overcoming an apparently insurmountable challenge. But I'd argue that his massive love of performing drives him even more. You can see the joy he gets when he's entertaining someone, whether with his motorcycle mastery, by playing guitar in a small gathering, or when he is recreating funny or exciting experiences with his entertaining anecdotes.

In the fall of 1976, Doug learned of a traveling carnival set up in the parking lot of a nearby department store. "Perfect," he thought. Here was his opportunity to bring his new love of bicycle jumping to the masses attending that carnival.

Doug and Arthur loaded up the bicycle, wooden ramps, carpenter's saw-horses, and cement blocks into and on top of Arthur's large 1970s Chrysler and headed out to that carnival. Surprisingly, no one objected to the idea, so Arthur parked his car and two others side-by-side, as close as possible. They then constructed ramps and carefully placed them on each end of the hoods of the cars, using plywood, sawhorses, and cinderblocks. A large crowd gathered, having never seen anything like this before. Doug performed several of his trademark wheelies and then rode his bicycle far off in the distance to get a good run towards the plywood ramps.

Off in the distance, you could see this 14 year-old, gangly kid, his long blonde hair sticking out of the gold, metal-flaked three-quarter motorcycle helmet (which was the only protective gear he wore), turn his bike around and begin pedaling toward the takeoff ramp at a blistering pace. He was pedaling with fierce determination and his handlebars swung from left to right, left to right, over and over again. You could see the bicycle's big banana seat and a raised sissy bar rocking back and forth like an upside-down clock pendulum. This frantic pace kept up right up to the point where he hit the takeoff ramp, which was nothing more than a flimsy piece of plywood leaned against a carpenter's sawhorse and reinforced in the middle with the cinderblocks.

In an instant, accompanied by the gasps of the now large crowd, he launched over the hoods of those cars. As quickly as it started, it ended with a hard but smooth landing. After sailing over the hoods of the vehicles, Doug planted the bicycle perfectly on the precarious plywood set up on the other side. With a big grin, he flipped the bike around and wheelied back to the takeoff area to the cheers of the crowd. "Do it again, do it again," they chanted. Without hesitation, he rode off in the distance, turned the bike around, and simply repeated the feat. He reveled in the crowd's reaction. He was hooked; there would be no turning back for this natural, born performer.

Chapter 3
A Dream is Born

"If you have a dream and the willpower to pursue it, you can be whoever you want to be."
~ Doug Danger ~

Doug will be the first to tell you that his mother was his driving force and inspiration. "You can be who you want to be, but it's going to take hard work, grit, and determination," was her mantra.

It's not that she was genuinely thrilled about him pursuing a life as a daredevil; deep down, she would have preferred him to choose a safer profession. However, she fully supported and encouraged him because she was such a strong advocate for living the life you want and taking the opportunity to chase one's dreams. She loved Doug and was not going to stand in the way of a young man and his aspirations.

Broken Cars and Broken Lives

With that said, Doug had plenty of doubters and certainly had the opportunity to go down the wrong path by the time he hit high school.

It was the 1970s, and drugs were prevalent. Both of us vividly recall that the local drug dealer would, believe it or not, stand outside the local bank selling his wares if you wanted them. I assume he was well known to everyone. How on Earth could this go on in plain sight on a downtown street? I don't know, but it did. Perhaps because of this acceptance and the easy access, many of Doug's friends strayed down the wrong path.

To this day, with tears in his eyes and a knot in the pit of his stomach, Doug retells the story of his close high school friend who made the wrong choice one evening, and after taking drugs, decided to go for a joy ride in his newly acquired car.

Reportedly, the car was mangled and crumpled beyond recognition, as was his friend's body. The wake and funeral were, understandably, a closed casket affair.

When talking about his friend, Doug is inspired by the story Evel Knievel told about the famous Indianapolis Motor Speedway races and how some racers would try to cheat.

"There are some racers who try to put in cheater fuel to get an edge on their competition. Well, with that fuel, the cars will go much faster, but only for a little while before blowing all to hell. That's what happens to you with drugs. You will go a little faster until you blow yourself all to hell."

Doug took these words to heart, and to this day he has never touched or tried any drugs. Following in Evel's footsteps, and because he is so fervently against drug use, Doug continues the tradition of encouraging his young audience members to stay away from drugs.

Many thankful parents in attendance at his shows go out of their way to personally thank him and praise him for this speech and this stand. For Doug, their gratitude never grows old.

The late Evel Knievel even commented on Doug's stance after seeing his anti-drug speech at one of his performances. He thanked Doug and congratulated him for continuing the tradition he (Evel) began so many years before.

High School Hijinks

In his teens, with his family's encouragement, Doug dabbled in motorcycle hill climbing and motocross with some success. However, long-distance jumping and performing was always his goal.

Just like he did in his early years when he learned how to master a bicycle wheelie, Doug spent hour after hour honing his slow wheelie skills at his family's home in the driveway and down the town's nearby sidewalks on a borrowed motorcycle. Of course, many of his neighbors were not fans of his endless practicing, as evidenced by their sneers and complaints. Once he mastered the slow wheelie, high-speed wheelies became easier and safer.

When I asked him about his longest wheelie, he recalled with what can best be described as a Cheshire Cat grin, that he had done a six-mile wheelie on the Massachusetts Turnpike (US Interstate-90) on his off-road dirt bike in his high school years. "Most of the people in cars seemed pretty excited," he said. "They were beeping their horns and yelling words of encouragement... most—not all."

His most legendary devilish deed involving a motorcycle was, in a sense, a tribute to Evel Knievel. You see, for whatever reason, Doug decided that it would be a hoot to also ride his motorcycle through his high school while school was in session. He planned the logistics of the stunt with a couple of close friends, even determining the day, what "sickness" he would use for an excuse to be absent, and what time to do it. As the day approached, Doug very wisely had reservations and considered canceling the stunt. However, as word of the impending hijinks leaked out, the student body was already astir, wondering whether he would actually go through with it.

Briefly, Doug began to wise up a bit and have second thoughts. Obviously, there was a "mole" in the system, though, because word of Doug's flash of sensibility leaked out.

As the agreed-upon day neared, Doug recalls getting a visit from two twin brothers who were big bruisers and offensive linemen on the high school's varsity football team. He went on to say that one of them grabbed his shirt near one of his shoulders and dragged him to the side of the school's hallway, into an area just beyond the lockers. The two, at least a foot taller than Doug, pinned him up against the wall and forced him to bend his neck as far back as possible to look them in the eyes as they explained the reason for the chat.

To Doug's surprise, it turned out that the scuttlebutt over the planned exploit had resulted in some of the football players placing wagers, and these two brothers had wagered heavily on him going through with the feat.

I first learned of this high school shenanigan from the local radio station on my way home from a different, nearby high school (a trade school). His hallway hell-ride was all over the news. Perhaps he feared I might have talked him out of it, so he never revealed his intent to me. Nevertheless, as soon as I heard the news, I instinctively knew it was him, even though the authorities had not yet revealed the perpetrator!

The timing of the ride through the school's hallways couldn't have been worse (or better, depending on your take). You see, just as his accomplices on each end of the school held open the double doors, and just as a disguised Doug blasted his way up the school steps and into the hallway, the class bell rang. All the students rushed into the halls as they usually did. The chaos was maddening and could only be compared to the Running of the Bulls in Pamplona, Spain. Students screamed, scurried, and dived out of the way, as the dirt bike's two-stroke deafening *braaap* reverberated and echoed throughout the school like an angry bull.

Doug was understandably eager to make his way through the mass of students, while angry teachers and administrators chased him or stood in the way of him and his machine.

He made his way out of the exit doors (still propped open by his accomplices) with a leap halfway down the school's massive steps, and then quickly raced to the school gates and down the street, heading to his home to hide the evidence less than a mile away.

Not wanting to wake Arthur, who worked the graveyard shift and was still sleeping, he killed the motor as he neared his home, quietly rolled the bike into the yard, stashed the "evidence" in the garage, then made his way back to his room where he could innocently play sick again.

Unfortunately for this poor planner, who was a much better motorcycle rider and racer than he was a criminal, Palmer's finest were on the case. I wasn't the only one to immediately suspect Doug. The Palmer Police also had a sneaking suspicion as to the identity of the culprit and quickly made their way over to Doug's home, where one of the officers proceeded to awaken Arthur, yet again.

"What the hell do you want now?" Doug could hear Arthur blurt out to the officer. "No, he's been here the whole time… He did what?… Sure, you can check the garage."

As you might have suspected, the bike's engine was still hot, resulting in Palmer's finest closing the hell-ride case rather quickly and Doug being expelled permanently from his school by a terribly angry and apparently unforgiving school principal. And that's how Doug ended up going to the local trade school.

Fortunately, the judge at the local courthouse found some humor in the joyride and let Doug off with a, "You did, *what*?", a chuckle, and a short probation period.

Many years later, as a local celebrity and motivational speaker, Doug was invited back to address the student body at his former high school. Following his inspirational speech, he stayed around to greet individuals and autograph posters.

To his surprise, as the student body began to disperse, who should appear with a poster to be signed but the once angry principal, whom he hadn't seen since his high school days.

"Oh, hi Mr. Woods. Who should I make this poster out to?" Doug asked his former principal.

"Me, of course. I'm a big fan," a smiling Mr. Woods replied. Obviously, Principal Woods IS a forgiving man.

As a side note, I recently visited with the occupants of Doug's old home in downtown Palmer, where Doug drove his neighbors crazy learning how to wheelie in the driveway and on the sidewalks, and of course tried to stash his bike after the ride through the high school. When the opportunity was right, I revealed to the much younger owner that his was the house where Doug Danger had lived and the driveway where Doug Danger learned to wheelie.

His response? "Oh yeah, I heard all about Doug Danger from one of the police officers."

I guess you could say that Doug Danger's legend lives on in his hometown.

A Hometown Star

Having been thrown out of his first high school, Doug was forced to look for a different school. He chose to attend a local vocational trade school also in his hometown of Palmer. His attendance at that school was instrumental in his learning auto mechanics, and he was also able to get his first set of professional motorcycle ramps built by the carpentry department there.

With these ramps, Doug performed his first public jump after about a month of regular practice at a local entrepreneur's airplane landing strip. Unfortunately, this jump did not go as planned; it ended in a spectacular crash. It was his last major jumping crash until the devastating wreck in New Hampshire, 10 years later.

Except for a severe concussion, the crash resulted in no significant injuries, but it taught him a valuable lesson about being fully prepared to prevent such a thing from ever happening again. On the other hand, the crash made the front page of the hometown weekly newspaper, making Doug a bit of a local hero.

"In my eyes, I was a big star…at least for that week," Doug recalled with a laugh. "I loved it and wanted more."

Chapter 4
From The Minors To The Majors

"Success happens when determination becomes unstoppable"
~ **Doug Danger** ~

At 18 years old, Doug had already made a name for himself locally, and he started a traveling motorcycle thrill show known as Cycle Stunts Unlimited. Comprising of a group of Doug's friends and fellow stunt riders, Cycle Stunts Unlimited toured much of New England and New York State with Doug Danger as the star of the show. They put on many successful shows and navigated some steep learning curves, learning critical lessons amassing amusing stories along the way.

With no professional guidance, Doug headed out on the road that summer. The first stop was at Star Speedway in Epping, New Hampshire, for an event combining motorcycle flat track and automobile winged sprint cars, and of course Cycle Stunts Unlimited. From there, it was off to

Hudson Speedway in Hudson, NH, the track that would nearly take his life a decade later. There, Doug met Russ Conway, a track and events promoter. The two eventually became good friends and longtime business associates. Doug credits much of his later success to this relationship and Conway's encouragement.

The Bare Necessities

When Doug and I were discussing and developing this account of his life and career, he thought it was essential to emphasize that success is most often preceded by many mishaps, failures, and "learning experiences" while one is perfecting one's craft or starting a business venture. To steal a line from mutual friend Dennis A. McCurdy, "You're going to suck before you get good."

Suffice to say, that first full year was sprinkled with many challenges and learning experiences, from discovering how to become a strong leader, to building a strong team, and even a couple of embarrassing wardrobe malfunctions. Doug learned that show business, small business, and motorcycle thrill show ownership was a tribulation in itself and equally as difficult as the stunts themselves.

Speaking of various malfunctions, most people probably think celebrities don't ever have a bad day or that they never do anything incorrectly. That's because movie stars can just say "cut" and then move on to "take two" for another shot at doing a line or scene correctly. "Take one" is destroyed, and no one ever sees it. Well, for a risk-taker doing live shows, there's no such thing as another take. The crowd only gets to see the first attempt.

Take, for example, the time Doug packed his bags in a rush for a show in New Hampshire and forgot to pack underwear. Now, it's not a big deal to go "commando," but he was jumping in a rented tuxedo that day, and when he threw a leg over the bike, the whole backside of his pants ripped wide open. Unfortunately, with the bike running, Doug never heard the tuxedo pants tear. It wasn't until he was standing on the seat doing a wheelie that he felt a considerable draft and realized something was wrong. With one more wheelie to do while standing on the seat with one foot, Doug decided the show must go on, although he was unable to tell how bad the tear was. He landed the jump safely, but Doug gave a little more of a show than he'd planned on.

On a warm summer day at another show, Doug's bus was on the racetrack as the crew unloaded the ramps from the trailer attached to the bus. The stands were already full of thousands of spectators waiting for the event to begin. Doug had just unloaded the bikes and went into the bus to shower off. At the back of the bus, he stepped out of the shower and began toweling off. He was facing away from the crowd when suddenly he heard them clapping and cheering. He turned around, and saw to his mortification that the curtain on the grandstand side of the bus had broken and fallen to the floor. There he was, standing in front of tens of thousands of people in nothing but what God gave him at birth. To say he was embarrassed is an understatement. But being the consummate professional he is, he simply donned his leathers, gave an inspiring speech to the crowd, and performed one of his most incredible shows.

After the show, one of his crew members asked him, "How could you go out there and do a performance like that after such an embarrassing moment?"

Doug responded, "Life is like a poker game; it's not the cards you're dealt in life, but how you play them. You can win the whole pot of money with a pair of twos and a good poker face. Today, I had a great poker face."

The point Doug was trying to make was that life is not always champagne and caviar. Everybody has tough situations dealt to them once in a while. Being a winner in life is not about being able to win with four aces in your hand; it's about your attitude when life deals you a pair of twos. How do you react? Are you going to fold, or are you going all in? Doug has always been all in!

Souvenir Poster Circa 1980

Risk Turns to Danger

With all new business ventures comes a tremendous financial risk. For example, there's the dreaded rainout. The first year on the road seemed to be filled with more rainouts than shows. Rainouts equaled a significant financial loss for Doug, who was running his newly formed thrill show on a shoestring budget.

Rain notwithstanding, many of the events that year went off without a hitch, and most were well received by the promoters, track owners, and fans. With his sheer determination and free help from friends, he was able to complete his first full season and make a name for himself throughout the northeast United States. Additionally, that first year an enthusiastic local promoter dubbed him "Mr. Danger." And although Doug admits he never had the heart to tell this particular promoter that he spelled Evel Knievel's name wrong on the promotional material, that's how Doug Senecal, of Palmer, Massachusetts, became known as "Doug Danger."

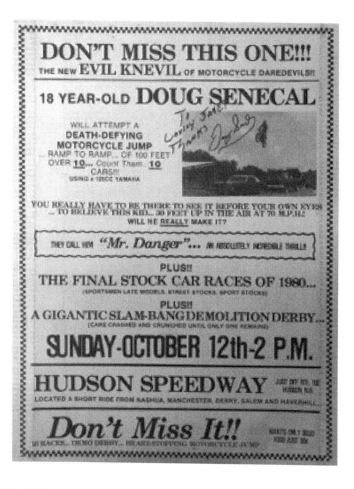

Building a Team

Despite his fame, and whether he is dealing with tragedies or celebrating triumph, Doug has always maintained a likable, friendly, fun, and humble personality. I'd argue that his success that first year and beyond was partly made possible due to these traits. Throughout his career, countless people have stepped up to support and assist him with his quest, many of them traveling great distances at their own expense or putting off other pressing issues just to help their friend. This support was evident early on and continues as he approaches the twilight of his career.

A likable person with a dream attracts talented individuals to his or her cause. This phenomenon has been demonstrated repeatedly in Doug's career and in other organizations worldwide. Doug will be the first to tell you that his success would not have been possible without a reliable team behind him. Yes, motorcycle jumping is eventually the individual accomplishment of one man flying a machine, but no leader is ever successful without the support of a reliable team.

In his motivational speeches, Doug emphasizes that a team approach has always been his key to success and is the key to leadership and any organization's success. He goes on to say that successful leadership requires sharing a vision and inspiring and cultivating each team member. He asserts that every one of us has a talent, or a specialty. Leaders must take time to recognize and identify individual skills, encourage people to participate, and then acknowledge each person's skillful contribution. This is the formula for growth and success.

During his first year, Doug and his thrill show had more than their share of trials, tribulations, and "valuable learning experiences." But Doug held his team of volunteers together by never losing his vision, dream, or kindness.

A Major League Tryout

At the age of 19, with the encouragement and help of promoter Russ Conway, Doug secured an audition with the renowned Joie Chitwood Automobile Thrill Show at the now closed Sunshine Speedway in Tampa, Florida, where the "Hell Drivers" were preparing for their upcoming season.

Starting in the mid-1940s, The Chitwood show was a regular at carnivals and fairs throughout America, where they performed hundreds of shows each year. Their performers were often the go-to automobile stuntmen called up to do a movie or television show stunt scene.

Russ Conway's advice to Doug before leaving: "Show him what talent you've got; look the part regardless; fake it till you make it; have first-class confidence."

In December of 1980, prepared to follow Conway's advice, Doug grabbed his only pair of custom made motorcycle racing leathers and his 1980 Yamaha YZ125 and cleaned and polished both. He then loaded them in his beat-up 1964 Ford pickup, which he had repainted himself, using a paintbrush and a couple of pails of black and yellow paint and to which he had added a brand new "YamaHauler" sticker on the rear window (which probably cost more than the truck). Figuring he'd visit with his family while he was in Florida, who had by then moved there, he made the trek from Massachusetts for a tryout with Chitwood as his replacement motorcycle stuntman.

As the interview (or rather, the "demonstration of his motorcycle prowess") loomed with the Chitwoods, Doug made his final preparations for the encounter. He buffed and waxed his motorcycle one more time and then carefully chained and locked it outside of his parents'

Florida home, as he readied for the Christmas holiday.

On Christmas morning, Doug went to retrieve wrapped presents from his truck. It was a beautiful Florida morning, and Doug was in a great mood. Once he'd grabbed the gifts, he rounded the home just to peek one more time at his newly waxed motorcycle. That's when he realized his pride and joy had been stolen. The only thing left was a cut chain. Doug was devastated, not just because of the loss of the bike, but because someone would steal his motorcycle on Christmas Day. It was a crushing blow. The authorities never retrieved the motorcycle. Thank God for family and for it being the season of giving and joy, because his mom came through and helped him finance another bike in time for the tryout with the Chitwoods.

By 1981, Joie Sr., the founder of the now Chevy Thunder Auto Thrill Show, had retired and passed the tradition into the good hands of his sons, Tim and Joie Jr. Tim was the leader of the Western Division and Joie Jr. ran the Eastern Division. Doug was to interview with and demonstrate his skills to the latter.

No motorcycle stunts are complete without the signature wheelie, and this was a stunt Chitwood expected. So after a brief verbal interview, Doug was asked to suit up and demonstrate his expertise.

Doug started with a slow wheelie, stopping and starting at will and rounding turns and circling in each direction in a tight pattern not more than six feet around. He performed each circle without dropping the front wheel and with the rear fender sometimes scraping the pavement as he precariously balanced the super quick Yamaha YZ125.

Doug would stop the bike completely for a moment as he carefully twisted the throttle, then tapped the rear brake in rapid succession, while using his head, knees, and arms as counter-weights and twisting the handlebars back and forth as needed to keep the bike headed in the direction he intended. This was a bike made to go fast, definitely not slow like this, and he had to maintain perfect balance in this man-and-machine ballet of sorts.

When he was through demonstrating his "bag of tricks," he made his way towards Chitwood, waving with a quick flick of the wrist. Then, in one fluid motion, with the front wheel still high in the air and the rear fender dragging on the pavement, he came to a complete stop and dropped the front wheel just a few feet from Chitwood.

Chitwood was noticeably amused. "Hey, that's really cool," he said, "I've never seen anyone wheelie like that, but can you do them any faster?"

"Sure," Doug responded, "I can do them at any speed."

So, with a swift kick of his right foot, he brought the bike to life again, twisted the throttle a couple of times, and headed off to the end of the speedway with a series of loud, quick *braaaps* as he shifted through the gears. At the end of the racetrack, he brought up a wheelie in first gear, and with the wheel still in the air, began shifting through the gears until he was in top gear and nearly at top speed. He whizzed past a smiling Chitwood in a flash. At the other end of the quarter-mile asphalt speedway, Doug dropped the wheel, turned around again, and repeated the feat of lifting the front wheel in low gear and shifting through the gears without dropping the front wheel, hitting top speed again as he approached Chitwood. As he passed, he nearly flipped over backward in 6th gear, but he tapped the rear brakes (never dropping the wheelie) and slowed back down to almost a stop before setting the front wheel down a little ways past an amazed and amused Chitwood.

Doug then eyed the motorcycle ramp that had been set up for him. He throttled up again, made his way to the end of the speedway one more time, raced towards the ramp, and leaped off— flying about 50 feet from ramp to ground. Without hesitation, he continued around the track to leap one more time. However, to put a little icing on the cake, he jumped off the same ramp, squeezed the tank hard with his knees, and demonstrated his new trick of removing both hands from the handlebars as if he was signaling a touchdown in American football.

Keep in mind that in 1981, long before the days of extreme riding, this action was absolutely unheard of. No one ever *intentionally* let go of their motorcycle's handlebars in flight.

Laughing hysterically, Chitwood exclaimed, "Hey, that's all pretty cool. I have never seen anything done like that before! You've got the job if you want it."

Chitwood hired Doug on the spot, and in 1981 he spent the entire season traveling with Chitwood's team.

He was a major league player now, getting groomed and taught by a group who were among the most skilled traveling thrill show entertainers in the world. Not since Buffalo Bill's Wild West Show, or Barnum and Bailey's Circus, had a traveling thrill show entertained more people in such a skillful manner as the Chitwoods. With them, Doug would learn that showmanship is a skilled craft. From that day forward, Doug learned that success starts with giving a professional performance that entertains. The Chitwoods taught him the art of showmanship and how consummate professionalism is the key to one's success. When you combine a professionally crafted show with likable entertainers, you strike gold.

Doug was already an approachable and likable person, but he learned that entertainment takes attention to detail and careful planning well beyond the preparation necessary to pull off a major stunt. The feats performed almost daily by the Chitwood Hell Drivers were stunts designed to entertain more than to just thrill. You see, when a team is on the road doing the same stunts repeatedly in city after city, the risk must be minimal for the show to go on. The risk was low, but the entertainment value was high. It had to be that way, and Chitwood showed Doug how to reduce risk while increasing entertainment value.

That year, the Chitwoods also taught Doug the importance of humility. Doug tells a story about how he became a little cocky and how someone, he's not sure who, told him that everyone participated in the clean-up, and if he didn't want to do the grunt work they would just find a motorcycle jumper in the next town. It was a humbling lesson in the importance of being an active part of a cohesive team. More importantly, no matter how essential you might think you are, someone else is always eager and hungry to take your place. Everyone is replaceable. Doug would carry these lessons with him throughout his career.

Circa 1981

Chapter 5
Reaching For The Stars

"Turning your dreams into reality takes having the courage to defy the odds."
~ **Doug Danger** ~

Forest Lake, Palmer, Massachusetts 1984

By 1983, at the age of 21, Doug already had his sights on setting world long-distance motorcycle jumping records.

Doug said that the motorcycle performer he succeeded in the Chitwood show, Todd Seeley, was an inspiration. Doug and Seeley had become good friends, each helping the other with jumping and stunt tips, tricks, and ideas. They stayed in touch as each worked toward making a place in the record books while touring in their own respective traveling thrill shows.

Motorcycle jumping enthusiasts understand motorcycle limitations such as engine size and capability. They recognize distance records in different classes: 125cc, 250cc, and the "open class," or the overall long-distance record. The *Guinness Book of World Records* only acknowledges the long-distance record, but enthusiasts understand the limitations of smaller cc bikes and the significance of the three distinct record categories.

In 1985, Doug aspired to the 125cc record. He reached out to his friends at the nearby Thompson Speedway in Thompson, Connecticut, for a location and a venue to set the record in this category.

With his years of experience, professional showmanship, and training, Doug set out to create a spectacular show. However, in reality, he was financially limited and lacked the means to build a new set of ramps for the world record attempt. As he described it, he was "a kid" with a hammer, nails, and a set of old wooden ramps who attempted to build extensions to those ramps in order to—for lack of a better word—"safely" leap the distance necessary.

Just as he began the task, a group of speedway employees, who had been watching him from afar, interrupted him.

"Stop," one called out with a chuckle, "let's take a look at what you need."

Doug knew what he needed, but he didn't have the means to accomplish it. These guys had the tools and supplies, but not the knowledge. Together, with a trackside welder and the necessary metal cutting tools, they built steel extensions at the height and length needed.

On September 1st, 1985, in front of a packed Thompson Speedway crowd, Doug Danger made his way around the ½ mile banked asphalt track on his Yamaha YZ125 at an amazing speed for a 125cc motocross bike.

For those unfamiliar with the sound of a 125cc two-stroke motocross motorcycle, it sounds like

10,000 crazed killer bees. The small engine spins at nearly 10,000 revolutions per minute at full throttle. And of course for a jump of this magnitude, Doug needed full throttle. With the throttle full on, Doug hit the newly built takeoff ramp straight and true and launched high into the air until he was nearly level with the fans cheering him from the upper stands. There, he instinctively tapped the rear brake to level the motorcycle at the apex of the flight and eyed the landing area. Moments later, he throttled again near the bottom of the descent to lower the back wheel for touchdown. He heard the familiar sound of the back wheel slamming down onto the landing ramp, followed by the front wheel touching down with a second thud. With a twitch and a wobble, the bike sprinted down the ramp as Doug fought to regain and maintain control, working to carefully slow the machine before he ran out of straightaway. Before even slowing, he heard the cheers of the more than 10,000 people in attendance who had just witnessed a 125cc motorcycle successfully leap over 14 school buses. The jump was officially measured at 129-feet, 6-inches, tying Evel Knievel's record of 14-buses.

14 bus jump - Souvenir Booklet 1986

Sharing the Limelight

Doug has consistently demonstrated that to be successful, it is imperative to be someone who attracts friends, followers, and fellow dreamers.

Moreover, he's shown the importance of being willing to accept assistance, input, and yes, constructive criticism. Doug has never lost sight of these values; he remains humble and friendly to everyone he meets, which is why those men stepped in to help him with his ramps, his dream, and the eventual accomplishment of this record. He remains grateful to them and the countless others over the decades who have been there when he needed them.

Bigger and Better

Over the next few years, Doug spent many months on the road, performing hundreds of shows at fairs and speedways in the United States and Canada. But he always dreamed of more significant accomplishments.

Long before 1988, Doug had moved away from using a 125cc motocross bike and had stepped up to consistently using a 250cc motocrosser as his everyday go-to bike for stunts and wheelies in his performances. But he also began experimenting with a new Honda CR500 after receiving two new motorcycles from his sponsor. In 1988, Doug decided to repeat some of the jumps that Evel Knievel accomplished over the years. Consequently, he reached out to his old friends at Thompson Speedway and proposed a 19-car jump sometime that year. They planned the event, and the leap went off without a hitch. In his usual way, Doug recalled with a laugh, "I wasn't smart enough to jump one more than Evel back then."

In 1988, his friend Todd Seeley jumped his motorcycle 246 feet to claim the overall long-distance motorcycle jumping record and a place in the *Guinness Book of World Records*. At that time, this distance was thought to be unobtainable.

This accomplishment lit a spark in Doug. "If he can do it, I can do it," he thought. After all, "We are all human beings; no one is super-human, and each of these daredevils puts his pants on one leg at a time." Moreover, the time he'd spent with the Chitwoods and Seeley, who had also been groomed by the Joie Chitwood Thrill Show, had demonstrated to him that seemingly impossible feats can be accomplished with minimal risk when you do them properly, with careful and calculated preparation and practice. Seeley was quoted as saying, "I'm not a daredevil, like Evel Knievel. I'm a professional stuntman, and every stunt I do is very precise, practiced, measured, and controlled" (*Society*, 1998).

Yes, long-distance motorcycle jumping world record attempts are obviously risky, but Seeley, whom Doug saw and respected as a very "careful risk-taker," had just demonstrated that these greater distances were possible.

Jumpin's a Pain in the Neck

By now, Doug was regularly jumping 10-11 cars almost weekly at venues throughout the northeast United States and beyond, with longer distances scheduled periodically.

In 1989 the Trans-Canadian Hell Drivers (a traveling Canadian auto thrill show who also performed at northern United States venues) invited him to leap over 20 cars at the famed Canadian National Exhibition in Toronto, Canada. It is rumored that this team entered and exited the US with their entire entourage by route of a rural cross-border dirt road somewhere in the Midwest in the middle of the night. Doug would make the proposed leap on a 250cc two-stroke Honda CR motocrosser.

However, the jump unfortunately did not go as planned.

After his masterful demonstration of wheelies, and his trademark pre-jump speech, Doug made his way to the end of the stadium to begin a series of "speed runs" toward the takeoff ramp. He practiced hitting the precise speed necessary to carry him over the 20 brand new Chevrolets safely, a distance of well over 120-feet, tip to tip, from takeoff to landing ramp.

Flying and landing safely over a distance like this on man-made wooden and steel ramps takes precise speed control that is difficult to master. Hence, after calculating proper speeds using a combination of math and his long-held knowledge and experience, Doug Danger uses a speedometer to help him maintain the proper speed when launching off his typical 10-foot-high takeoff ramp.

Leaving the takeoff ramp one mile per hour too slow will result in man and machine falling approximately 12 feet short of the ideal landing area near the top of the landing ramp. Leaving the takeoff ramp a mere two miles per hour too slow will result in a landing far short of the target, leading to a major crash, and an almost certain death.

On the other hand, going too fast has pitfalls as well. One mile per hour too fast projects the bike roughly 20 feet beyond the target—a grievous mistake, considering that the landing area gets significantly lower with each foot because of the angle of the landing ramp. Two miles per hour too fast will result in man and machine flying to the very bottom of, or well beyond the 10 foot-high, 48 foot-long landing ramp. The last scenario is like riding a motorcycle off a four-story building onto flat ground at 80 miles per hour, which would result in a very rough landing, to say the least.

Complicating matters was the design of the Canadian football stadium. The design did not allow for a long run to the takeoff ramp because there was no opening to exit the stadium with the motorcycle. So, Doug needed to get up to speed rapidly, and he did not have much distance in which to do so. He would be able to obtain full speed just as he approached the bottom of the takeoff ramp.

Doug made two speed runs, rapidly shifting through all six gears and glancing down at the speedometer just before getting to, then turning away from the takeoff ramp. Unlike other jumps, where he would be able to maintain a preferred speed for a comfortable distance before touching the takeoff ramp, here he would only be able to reach optimal speed for just a split second. This gave him a mere nanosecond to decide whether to proceed with the jump or abort it, keeping in mind that he would have to maintain the same RPMs until launch. This leap was certainly going to be more difficult than many others.

Nonetheless, after several speed runs he was satisfied that he would be able to obtain and maintain the speed necessary to leap safely over these 20 cars, so he gave a thumbs-up to the crowd, made his way back to the far end of the stadium, and began his final run to the takeoff ramp.

The noise of the crowd was drowned out by the rapid successions of *braaap*, *braaap*, *braaap* that the two-stroke machine made as it went through its gears. Doug made his way toward the takeoff ramp. He hit 6th gear before quickly glancing down at his speedometer, and then he looked back up to be sure he was straight on the takeoff ramp's stripes. He glanced down to check the speedometer again, and at that instant he realized he was going too fast. He launched into the Toronto night sky at nearly 80 miles per hour.

Unless you've been there, it's difficult to understand the sinking feeling you get when you see your intended landing target, then the entire landing ramp, pass under your feet as you fly past. Time slows to a crawl, and you prepare for what you know is going to be an incredibly rough touchdown. Your heart races faster. Your chest tightens with tension as a rush of adrenaline enters your veins. Fear takes hold, and you fight to prepare for the inevitable but unknown consequences.

You see, the angle of the landing ramp plays an important role in making each leap smooth and safe. Yes, motocross bikes in 1989 had long suspensions—10 inches or so—but even today's machines cannot absorb the incredible pounding of a flat ground landing from 40 feet in the air. The impact was devastating. The suspension was unable to absorb the blow; it bottomed out almost immediately before transferring the remainder of the impact's force to Doug himself. He squeezed the tank with his knees, keeping them flexible to use them as another suspension, and gripped the bars with all his might. But it was too much for his body to take. He felt a pop, then an incredible pain in his neck and a strange, unfamiliar tingling in his limbs. He would later learn that the impact has snapped a vertebra in his neck.

He carefully slowed the Honda CR250, using what strength he had left. Then he turned the bike around and strained to raise his left hand to the crowd as he passed them, the cars, and the ramps. He tried to smile and be gracious about their hospitality and their cheers, but he was unable to stop to talk to the announcer out of fear that he would not be able move either of his feet off the pegs once he stopped. At least that was his worry, having never experienced this strange feeling in his limbs before.

Instead, he rode past and over to his truck, where he simply leaned the bike up against it and pressed the engine kill-switch with his left thumb. He was still unable to move either foot off the foot pegs.

Although he tried to demonstrate a positive attitude, it was clear to many around him that he was in distress. In fact, the ambulance crew on standby immediately flipped on their lights and drove over to him. The crew helped Doug off the bike and transported him to the nearest hospital, where he spent the next eight hours waiting to be seen, until he could wait no more.

A Man of His Word

Doug had another show scheduled two days later in his hometown, a day's drive away. He left the emergency room with a crew member who had joined him there. He and his crew then made the painful trek back to his home state. Each bump on the New York State Thruway (Interstate-90) was a painful reminder of how far he was from his destination and the local hospital there. His goal was to get patched up there and begin preparation for the next show—an 18-car jump at a venue owned by his good friend, Russ Baker.

At his hometown hospital, he was diagnosed with a small break in a neck vertebrate. They gave him a neck brace and ordered him not to lift or work, and certainly not to jump. However, Russ had put up $5000 to promote the next day's scheduled jump. Not wanting to let him down, Doug decided to head over to the venue and practice jumping while wearing the neck brace. He gave it his best shot, but couldn't jump with the neck brace, as it was too restrictive. So, he took off the brace and managed to complete the feat several times without any pain or tingling sensations. The show would go on as scheduled…and it did, without a hitch.

Why on Earth would he take such a risk? As Doug put it, "There's no way I was going to let my friend down. Yes, I could have been paralyzed. But, if you give your word, you keep it."

"We don't see that today as we did in the past," he continued. "We need to get back to that. If you say you are going to be somewhere, be there. If you say you are going to do something, do it."

One for the Record

Despite this setback and his awakening to the concepts of vulnerability and risk, Doug still pinned his sights on world records—especially the overall long-distance record held by his friend Todd Seeley.

In 1990, the former Bryar Motorsports Park in Loudon, New Hampshire, had become New Hampshire International Speedway (NHIS) and was under new management. Doug approached them shortly after their opening and asked them if they wanted him to break the world record at the new speedway. They hired him on the spot. During the world-famous Laconia Bike Week that same year, Doug cleared twenty-five cars, covering 181-feet, 6-inches, on his Honda CR250, breaking the 250cc world record.

As this was long before NASCAR came to the speedway, he drew the biggest crowd ever seen at NHIS. Almost as soon as he landed, event organizers sought him out to sign for the next year's (1991) bike week. Together, they decided that this would be his attempt at breaking the overall world record of 246 feet. He signed the contract that day and had one year to prepare for a leap once considered impossible.

Doug's first course of action was to elicit the help and expertise of his good friend and well-respected factory motorcycle mechanic, Mark Pluta. When Doug asked for advice regarding preparing his new Honda CR 500cc two-stroke motocross motorcycle for the jump, Mark's response surprised him.

Mark listened closely to Doug regarding his requirements for the planned world record attempt, and then responded, "You ain't never getting to the other side with a stock bike—not jumping that far! It's going to need a complete overhaul; I mean everything."

Mark then went on to name modifications and high-performance parts he deemed necessary to complete such a feat. These included:

- Porting and polishing the cylinder
- Installing high-performance reed valves
- Installing a high-performance expansion chamber (part of the exhaust system)
- Modifying the transmission with a higher top (5th) gear
- Adding a smaller sprocket on the rear wheel and a larger front sprocket
- Re-valving the suspension to withstand the tremendous impact
- Switching out both tires to handle the high speeds

"And that's just to start," Mark stated.

This list took Doug by surprise. He was almost afraid to ask, but responded with, "Okay … what's all this going to cost?"

Mark paused for a second, and then with a grin he responded, "You buy the parts, and after you land this thing, we're going out for drinks on your tab!"

Doug was both relieved and honored by Mark's reply and said with a laugh, "You're a tough negotiator!"

Knowing that his motorcycle was in good hands, Doug turned his attention to the other important details.

He had new ramps built, and practiced for the world record attempt at his favorite go-to location: Thompson Speedway, in Thompson, Connecticut.

Jumping in that 5/8-mile oval racetrack, while starting outside the speedway to gain extra speed, Doug was able to work his way up to leaps of 180 feet.

In recalling this story, Doug laughed and explained with wide eyes and a wider smile that, to be able to safely get up to speed before entering the speedway, he'd go into the parking lot as far as he could until it met a nearby rural road. From this road, a passerby was able to get a fairly good, unobstructed view of the racetrack.

During one of his practices, a passerby got out of his car and waved Doug over to him. Doug saw him, rode up, and killed the engine to talk to the excited man.

"Dude, I just want to tell you that you just made day, my life! I've never seen anything like that," the man exclaimed.

"That's what I love about performing," Doug laughed, "He made my day, too. I love hearing that from fans."

Even using the massive parking lot at Thompson Speedway, 180-feet was the longest distance he could leap and still keep it "safe" (his words, not mine).

His final practice jumps took place at NHIS. Here, he worked his way out to a distance that put the ideal landing target at 220 feet and repeated this feat several times at speeds now approaching close to 95 miles per hour.

Let me take a moment to discuss what this kind of speed does to a motorcycle designed for a motocross track and definitely not designed to travel anywhere near 100 miles per hour. These bikes, especially topped with an exposed rider, are not at all aerodynamic. They are twitchy and begin to dance and wobble at around 80 miles per hour. As miles per hour increase beyond that, so does the twitching, dancing, and wobbling. It is an extremely unsettling experience, even for a seasoned rider.

Not long ago I experienced this on a dual sport bike I was riding to work. For a full two weeks (10 workdays) I commuted about 50 miles from central Massachusetts to a Boston suburb by way of Interstate-90 on what is basically a 450cc dirt bike. Even with my 40-plus years of motorcycle riding and extensive racing experience, for the entire two weeks I found it impossible to settle in and relax at 80 miles per hour.

For me, it is unimaginable to think that someone could experience this twitching, dancing, and wobbling, while simultaneously flying nearly the length of an American football field. Nonetheless, this had become "routine" for Doug Danger. I find that utterly astonishing!

What is also astonishing is the number of cars that were lined up, side-by-side, for the world record attempt during Laconia Bike Week in 1991—42 brand new Chevrolets! To this day, this stands as the most (side-by-side) cars ever jumped successfully.

Doug wowed another massive crowd of motorcycle enthusiasts and Doug Danger fans with his motorcycle mastery, charm, and skill with a microphone in his hands. The fans were ready for what was to be a historic day—a day when they would witness a feat that had never been attempted before.

The weather conditions were just perfect and the crowd was in a frenzy. Doug made his speed runs up to and past the massive takeoff ramp and the equally enormous landing ramp at speeds approaching 100 miles per hour on that beautiful, warm, sunny New Hampshire day, readying himself for what would be either his most triumphant accomplishment or his most tragic failure. Each time, he looked down, quickly checking his speed, just before turning away from the approach to the takeoff ramp at the very last moment. Each time, he squeezed the tank with his knees and tightly gripped the handlebars to limit the twitching, dancing, and wobbling of a bike never designed to go even half that speed.

Finally, he was ready to go. This attempt would be thirty or more feet longer than he had ever flown before. He gathered up his courage, said a prayer, and waved to the crowd. He also waved to his wife and crew, who nervously watched Doug's demeanor and tried to gauge his mood. Then, he began to round the one-mile oval speedway counterclockwise, ever so slowly, until he reached the backstretch. Turning his head to the left as far as he could, he once more surveyed the task that faced him, and then began the familiar run through the gears. *Braap*, shift, *braap*, shift, *braap*, shift... he worked the massive 500cc two-stroke through the gears. Reaching and rounding turn four of the speedway, he glanced down at the speedometer and saw that he had surpassed the 90 mile per hour mark. He gently rolled the throttle even more. The next time he looked at the speedometer he had surpassed 95 miles per hour, and the takeoff ramp was rapidly approaching. It was imperative to get to and maintain the 98 miles per hour he had calculated to be the correct speed. He threw another glance at the speedometer, followed by a quick glance to see the front tire of the Honda touch the stripes of the takeoff ramp. He squeezed the tank even harder, readied his knees, head, and arms for launch, and in an instant soared into the sky just short of 100 miles per hour. As he left the takeoff ramp, he got his first glimpse of the landing ramp on the opposite side. There, he was able to eye his expected landing "sweet spot" somewhere near the top of the ramp, but far enough down to claim a new record, if he was lucky, skilled, and strong enough to hang onto the bike at landing.

As quickly as it began, it ended. At 98 miles per hour, a flight of that distance takes just a few seconds. With the front wheel just slightly higher than the rear wheel, it appeared to be a smooth landing, although it's never really smooth after flying these distances.

With a thud, the back wheel touched down, followed by the front wheel. Instinctively, Doug knew immediately that he had not flown far enough. He raised his salute to the crowd for their support and cheers, reached turn one of the speedway, and began to mentally prepare himself for another leap as he turned left to reverse course and announce his intention. However, to his surprise and disappointment, a crew member was standing on the landing ramp, pointing to what he claimed was the touchdown spot. However, that crew member had mistakenly indicated the wrong spot.

"I knew they marked it wrong," Doug recalled. "I wanted to just turn around and get ready to jump again." But by then, the announcer had already enthusiastically proclaimed a new world record. With that announcement, the fans immediately swarmed onto the speedway. "With all this going on, there was no way I could get them cleared and retry," Doug recalled with a sigh.

A local TV station reported the error. They had clear video evidence of the actual landing spot just short of the 247 feet needed to break the old record.

So, with the crowd gone, Doug went back the following week with friends, his mechanic, and the people needed to confirm a Guinness World Record.

"With no crowd there, I had time to be careful," he explained. That wording seems way out of place for something like this, but that's what you get from Doug. "So, I did six to seven jumps that day."

"The next-to-last jump was marked at 251 feet, but out of fear they might have marked the wrong spot again, I went one more time."

Leaving the ramp at 101 miles per hour, he flew 265 feet, landing at near the bottom of the landing ramp. The impact was so brutal that it immediately snapped his left wrist on impact, sending him into an uncontrollable wobble resulting in a horrifying crash. Amazingly, the left wrist break was the only serious injury he sustained in that fall.

After that, the 251-foot leap had to stand. It was reviewed, and after careful consideration was certified as a world record, which held up for nine years.

Never Losing Touch

Even with all these accomplishments under his belt, though, Doug was still unsatisfied with one aspect of his life: his relationship with his biological father. He wanted more, and continued to reach out to his dad. The two reconnected and stayed in touch by phone, speaking almost weekly. Doug, to his credit, never gave up on the man he had been close to as a young child, living in Las Vegas. Thanks to these efforts and perhaps his father's increasing fragility as he aged, the two grew close and spent time visiting each other when Doug's schedule allowed. Doug felt as though he was whole again. His father promised to relinquish the past and be there for Doug from then on.

Chapter 6
It's Getting Serious Now

"Dreams are for those who dare. Don't ever lose sight of those dreams. But know, with dreams come nightmares. Having the wherewithal to overcome these nightmares is where true courage is found."
~ **Doug Danger** ~

I asked Doug if he had any regrets. "Yes," said Doug. "We all know the risk, but so many died or were severely injured trying to beat that world record. That hurts. I hated to see that."

With a jump-off against his friend Robbie Knievel as the ultimate goal, Doug reached out to him on several occasions but was not satisfied with the response. So he began to challenge him at each television appearance, daring him at each opportunity.

In the interim, Doug was able to book a jump-off with Australian motorcycle jumping legend and movie stuntman, Dar Davies, at the New Hampshire Motor Speedway the following year.

To Doug's surprise, Davies arrived with only a 2-foot wide, 6-foot high takeoff ramp and no landing ramp. Davies was expecting to use Doug's landing ramp.

"It was nuts," Doug recalled. "My landing ramp was 4-feet higher than his takeoff ramp."

The competition would start at 100-feet and move up from there. Scoring would be determined by accuracy, with a bullseye painted on the landing ramp. One point would be lost for each foot the bike landed away from the target. A flip of a coin before each distance determined the order. The jumper with the lowest score at the end of the competition would win.

Both daredevils had successful jumps at the 100-foot and the 125-foot marks. Finally, the gap was stretched to 150-feet. A flip of the coin determined that Davies, who was leading in points, would leap the 150-foot gap first.

Doug said, "He seemed to be scared shitless. He nervously admitted to me in the pits, moments before the 150-foot leap, that he had never jumped anywhere close to that distance. I was scared for the guy. Yet he grabbed his helmet, kicked over his bike, and with a nod, headed onto the track for what was to likely be his final run."

Davies fell short and landed on what is known as the "safety ramp," an 8-foot flat extension of the landing ramp to prevent instant death in the event someone does come up short of the "sweet spot" on the landing ramp. It is not intended as a landing area, and many times does not prevent a crash. Yet Davies was able to wrestle the bike to a stop without a mishap.

Under the rules, a landing on the safety ramp was not considered a valid jump. So the announcer said to him, "The judges have decided that if you want to go again, you may, as this jump doesn't count."

Without hesitation, Davies exclaimed over the loudspeaker, "Go to hell! I ain't going again unless you pay me double."

Then it was Doug's turn. On his final attempt, he landed his rear tire perfectly in the bullseye and was subsequently declared "World Champion."

L to R, Dar Davis, Andy White, and Doug Danger

"It was then that I realized I had reached a plateau that few daredevils had. I looked up to Davies and others, but I had attained a point where they couldn't match what I was capable of. I had also achieved a peak where even the best were scared. I saw it on his face, and that scared me." It had become serious business, with grave consequences for failure.

In less than a week came the calls he'd been waiting for. First, it was Robbie Knievel's agent, ready to talk. Then he received a call from the promoter who could make it happen: $250,000 guaranteed for a pay-per-view jump-off against Knievel. But less than two weeks after being declared World Champion, Doug Danger,

Guinness Book of World Records motorcycle long-distance jump record holder, would be lying in a coma clinging to life after crashing head-on into the first turn wall at New Hampshire's Hudson Speedway.

Chapter 7
The Long Road Back

If today the jump shall win and I do not return, I will go to my grave content knowing I've done my best, tried my hardest, and lived my life the way it was meant to be.
~ Doug Danger ~

The bright white light was blinding, burning. As quickly as it came, it disappeared, then returned, even brighter and more blinding. It flashed in one eye, then the other. Then he heard the distant, faint voices, and one male voice distinctly calling his name as the white light flashed again.

He strained to focus on the bright light and realized the voices were coming from the same direction. Confused, he pondered: "Do I resist? Do I go to the light? Do I acknowledge the voices? Who are they, and why are they calling my name?" He struggled to understand.

Realizing he had little choice, he resisted no more, allowing his consciousness to travel towards the light and the voices.

He struggled to open and focus his eyes. He observed a sterile, white room with bright lights and lots of strange, mechanical sounds.

Before his eyes was a man dressed in white, holding a brightly lit object in his right hand. He seemed friendly and not at all threatening as he looked at Doug intently.

Others in the room also seemed friendly and happy to see him, each sporting broad smiles as they looked upon him.

A middle-aged woman in what appeared to be a loose-fitting, light blue uniform was smiling but not speaking.

He then felt a gentle caress on his head. He slowly turned his head to the right to see a beautiful, much younger blonde woman, dressed in street clothes. She looked familiar. She greeted him with a, "Hi, honey," but he couldn't place where he'd seen her before.

"Why are these people here? Why am I here? Where am I?" He wondered, still confused but not fearful. He continued to survey their reactions and the room.

"Mr. Senecal? Can you hear me, Doug?" The man in white asked with a warm smile. "Welcome back. How are you feeling? I'm your doctor," he stated, as he again held the light up and flashed it in Doug's eyes.

After waking from the coma, Doug Danger spent six more weeks in a rehab center receiving occupational, physical, and speech therapy before being released to his home. Because of the coma, he had lost all of his memories. He didn't even know who his family was. Doug had no recollection that he was married and that the blonde woman caressing his head in the hospital was his wife. Who *he* was, was wholly lost to him.

Over the next few months at the rehab center, (and over the next couple of years at home), Doug had to relearn all the functional abilities he had acquired as a child, from walking (at first with a walker), to processing thoughts and speaking clearly. Everyday tasks that he had once taken for granted had become a struggle to learn and do. The severe brain injury, sustained in that horrifying crash at New Hampshire's Hudson Speedway months ago, had wiped him clean of every memory and almost every essential functional ability. Basically, he was like a child beginning life. He had to "grow up" again, struggling at first to learn to speak, walk, and groom himself. He also had to relearn the difference between right and wrong, morals, laws, and much later how to drive. He slowly progressed from a second childhood to adulthood once again.

As time went on, he was introduced to strangers who once were friends and family. He had no recollection of ever knowing many of them. But with time, as his brain healed, bits and pieces of those memories began to return.

Those times were tough for Doug, and as he put it, "It was a terrible head injury; everyone treated me like a child, like I was different. I was slow, socially awkward, and had to learn to do even the simplest things all over again. When you are slow in an adult's body, you get picked on because people think you are stupid. That's when you discover who your friends truly are."

During these painful years, Doug described being bullied, mocked, and ridiculed. "It hurt so bad. I know what it's like to be bullied. I lived it. I even contemplated suicide to kill the pain of the bullying, but I eventually learned that to give up is not the answer; the answer is to outsmart them instead. They are the problem, not you."

Today, Doug Danger is most proud of the speeches he gives to school children on the dangers of bullying and how to prevent it.

"This may sound sappy, but a pivotal moment in my recovery came while I was watching [the animated movie] 'The Lion King' (Roger Allers, 1994), which came out at the time I was recovering," Doug recalled with a smile. "The young lion, Simba, looks at his reflection in the puddle and then sees his deceased father, who states to his son, 'Remember who you are.' I immediately began to choke up. I had forgotten who I was. While at the hospital and rehab center, people would ask me for an autograph, and at first I was unsure why. I decided at that time to learn exactly who I was."

Doug enlisted the help of his brother Mike to obtain memorabilia, photos, and videos of his past. "Mike sent me a video of my crash and other jumps. I thought, 'That is cool as heck! That is who I was and who I want to be again!'"

Even now, Doug has no memory of hitting the wall, and thankfully little memory of the pain he lived with during his recovery.

But why would he ever jump again after such a devastating injury and the years of rehabilitation, even if he doesn't recall the pain?

Doug explained, "Anyone who had a motorcycle crash that bad would have likely not gotten back on. I went back to jumping because I didn't want to be known as a slow, stupid has-been. I wanted to be somebody. So, I called some friends to help me set up my ramps for the first time in three years. I was hooked again!"

On the Wings of an Angel

Unimaginably, and to the amazement of even the most optimistic healthcare professionals, Doug was able to crawl back to be the man he is today. More importantly, and more incredibly, he went on to become a better professional performer and an even better, kinder person.

How? Doug later professed that, somewhere between Hudson Speedway and the Trauma Center, he believes he was touched by an angel—that a true miracle happened. Certainly

Arlene Shea, that trauma nurse who saved his life, was an earthy angel to whom he is forever indebted. But there was more; there had to have been. After all, his heart had stopped for nearly 30 minutes.

Yes, Arlene and the ambulance crew pounded on his chest diligently the whole time. Still, many healthcare professionals will tell you that it is nearly impossible for anyone to recover from that; a heart cannot stop for 30 minutes without some lasting brain damage occurring. And although his close friends will argue that you'd *have* to be brain damaged to do what Doug Danger still does, there is little clinical evidence that he suffers any deficits to this day—a real miracle, some would say.

Recovery took years—many years—but with faith, support from his family, and sheer grit and determination, Doug Danger believes he also learned who he was destined to be. As he put it, "Being the average Joe wasn't me. I was born to be Doug Danger."

And the jump-off and all that money?

"I wasn't ready to handle all that money at that time. I have no regrets," Doug said with his infectious smile.

Losses like No Others

"Hey, I haven't called my father in a while," Doug blurted out one day during his long recovery. "I think I'm going to give him a call."

"Doug, I don't know how to tell you this, but your dad died three weeks before your Hudson Speedway crash," Tina responded.

"I grieved all over again," Doug recalled. "It was heartbreaking and shocking."

The years of recovery also took a toll on Doug and Tina's marriage.

"I put her through a lot. She worked long, hard hours to support our family during my recovery," he stated. During his recovery their family had grown with the addition of a second child, a baby boy.

"It was taking a toll on her. Having me to deal with was like raising a grown kid. I had mood swings and sometimes suffered from boredom. I was home and struggling daily to scratch my way back while she worked long hours every day. Our relationship became strained. I don't blame her for being angry or frustrated."

He continued, "In the end, we both fell out of love, but it was my idea to end the marriage. To this day, we remain good friends and co-parents. I'm grateful that we remained close. We always wish each other well and help each other out. The relationship we continue to have really helped me improve. I knew my family was going to be okay. That made my mental health better and paved the way for a complete recovery. I was looking forward to the future."

No Earthly Explanation

"I was in a really bad place emotionally by the time I made what was supposed to be my triumphant return to Hudson Speedway four years after the crash," Doug recalled. "And, sure enough, it was windy as hell—even worse than the day I crashed."

He said the place haunted him. "I knew that if I was going to make it as a jumper again, first I had to go back to Hudson Speedway and complete that jump. I had to!"

Eyewitnesses that day acknowledge that the wind was steady and blowing extremely hard from the backstretch side of the track toward the grandstand. All the attendees noted the giant American flag on the track's infield, and how Old Glory was violently blowing straight out all day.

"I was supposed to jump during the halftime intermission, but kept pushing it off because of the wind," Doug confessed. "I admit I was scared. I had just spent four years of recovery after crashing hard at this place. It nearly cost me my life. Now, I found myself back there with even crappier conditions than I had seen four years earlier. I was angry at myself and the weather."

For the first time in his life, Doug was seriously considering calling off a jump.

As Doug recalls, he watched the wind conditions throughout the day, and as the races started to wind down, the promotor approached him and stated, "You know, you aren't getting paid if you don't jump." Doug knew he needed to decide.

With a renewed determination to overcome his nervousness, he gave the affirmation to his crew to start setting up the ramps. He was going to go through with the jump.

Doug recalled the scene, "That friggin' flag was still out straight the whole time," he demonstrated the flag whipping horizontally in the wind with his hand, "flapping" his fingers.

The crowd in attendance for this monumental comeback was collectively holding its breath, equally mindful of the high winds and the challenge they would pose.

Once the ramps were up and the crew took their places, Doug performed his usual display of wheelies and speed runs, but he decided to forgo his routine of riding up the takeoff ramp. Instead, he somberly walked up. As he stood at the top of the takeoff ramp, he slowly glanced down to survey the 11 race cars lined up side-by-side, first looking down at the nearest car below his feet, and then slowly raising his head as he studied each subsequent car until the landing ramp came into his view. The landing area seemed strangely far away that day.

With the steady wind still feverishly howling, he glanced beyond the landing ramp. Here, the solid cement wall of turn one came into view—

the same one he had so violently collided with four long years earlier. That wall had changed his life drastically. He was fuming mad at himself and the world.

"You told me you were always going to be there for me, Dad. Where are you now?" He raised his head to the sky and cried out as he worked to shake off the intense feeling of doom.

"I got on the bike, fired it up, gave a loving nod to my brother Mike, and set off around the track to gain the speed I needed for the jump," Doug continued. "As I rounded the fourth turn, that flag was still straight out, flapping in the wind, but I stayed on the throttle and readied myself for the jump."

"I was scared to death for him," recalled Dean Sasen, his friend and crew member. "He asked me my opinion on going through with the jump, and I told him to call it off. I didn't want to walk this Earth knowing my opinion was what brought an end to the baddest motorcycle daredevil since Evel Knievel."

Dean continued, "I have no clue why I'm here, or what will happen next in this mad world, but I do know this: there are people in my life who can testify to some pretty cool, extraordinary events. I know the power of God, and I witnessed a miracle that day." He excitedly retold the story: "I saw it. I saw Old Glory, with the constant wind blowing at least 35 miles per hour that day. Then I saw the front tire touch the takeoff ramp and watched that flag immediately drop to a dead still at that exact moment. Through the silent air he flew. As soon as he touched down on the landing ramp, Old Glory immediately went straight out again, like a picture-perfect stance. A frickin' miracle. There's no other explanation. God was there with him."

And everyone in the crowd that day saw the "frickin' miracle" with their own eyes, too.

"But, wait," I said to Doug. "How did you know? *Did* you know? Why would you jump in those conditions? It's typically suicide."

"I got to the top of the ramp," Doug replied. "In anger, I scolded my father. Then I heard it, plain as day, just like I'm talking to you… 'Just go. I got this. Just go.' I heard my dad say it. It was his voice. I'd know it anywhere. So I went, and sure enough, he was there for me!"

That day affirmed to Doug, and perhaps to most of those in attendance, that Heaven is much closer to us than we sometimes think, and just maybe miracles and guardian angels aren't entirely a myth. Nevertheless, "luck" aside, Doug would eventually find that one must learn to keep confidence in check.

One Step at a Time

Doug's first "big jump" as part of his comeback came in the Fall of 1999, when he was to jump over 18 tractor-trailer trucks at Sam Boyd Stadium in Las Vegas. It was to be another record-breaking leap, surpassing his friend Robbie Knievel's 17 tractor-trailer truck record.

Doug described being genuinely concerned in practice as he was approaching the distance of 150 feet, give or take (depending on how close the trucks were parked together), he needed to clear the 18 trucks for the stunt that evening.

"I brought the distance out to 110 feet and was consistently getting terribly crossed-up. It was so bad that I felt like I'd be sideways or backward by the time I took it out to 150 feet. Despite every attempt to fix the problem, I was unable to correct it," he recalled. "Around that time, I had just had my fourth surgery on my right wrist and had no strength at all. At takeoff, I was overcompensating to hang on with my left wrist, and it was causing me to cross up."

Doug continued, "My brother Mike was there, and I said to him, 'I can't do this, Mike. I'm going to be backwards by the time I get to 150 feet.'"

"Okay," Mike said. "You just did 110 feet consistently, and you held on. Can you hang on at 120 feet?"

Doug went on, "So I said yes, and I did. I jumped 120 feet, crossed up the same, but no more, no less."

He finished the story by saying that he eventually practiced out to 150 feet, was able to hang on despite still crossing up, and went on to perform the same stunt in front of the Las Vegas fans.

"Mike kept telling me to forget the eventual goal of 150 feet. Focus on one step at a time, or in my case, 10 feet [longer] at a time."

This reminder was a valuable lesson that helped keep Doug in check emotionally for that stunt. Moreover, it also can be a lesson in life for all of us. Goals and dreams may seem overwhelming and unobtainable when you first conceive them, leading to a paralysis of sorts that keeps you from ever taking that first step towards them.

Doug did have a valid reason for his doubt and fear. After all, his experience had taught him that jumping motorcycles was a serious business with serious consequences. Nonetheless, he had also experienced thousands of successful jumps. Moreover, he was one of the best, if not *the* best, motorcycle stuntmen in the world. A successful jump for him over these 18 tractor-trailer trucks required overcoming doubt and fear (pushing these thoughts to the back of the brain), identifying weaknesses (his wrist injury causing the cross-ups), and deciding on a one-step-at-a-time plan of action.

Going into that jump, doubt and fear were starting to paralyze Doug. He was at the point where he needed to decide how important this line of work was to him. This tractor trailer jump in Las Vegas was his opportunity for a big comeback, and big dollars were on the line. To walk away would have been devastating to his career and reputation.

With much-needed support and encouragement, he was able to focus on accomplishing each "next step" in the process, which eventually led him to achieve the entire goal and overcome his doubt and fear.

Chapter 8
Confidence Turns to Calamity

Never forget who you are, where you started, and what you believe in. It may save your life someday.
~ Doug Danger ~

By 2004, Doug had teamed up with Tim Chitwood (the brother of Joie Chitwood Jr.), fellow motorcycle daredevil Louis "Rocket" Re, and thrill show clown turned auto stunt daredevil Justin Bellinger to form the "Legends Stunt Show." This group of motorcycle and auto hell drivers toured much of the United States east of the Mississippi, performing hundreds of shows a year.

L to R, Scott Senecal, Doug Danger, Justin "Wrong-Way" Bellinger, Tim Chitwood, and Lou "Rocket" Re of the Legends Stunt Show team

During these years, Doug described himself as beginning to gain confidence, and maybe sometimes becoming over-confident. For example, he explained that performing in conditions that were "less than ideal" was commonplace. Sometimes he even performed in downright sloppy weather conditions.

"But if we wanted to get paid, the show had to go on," Doug explained.

One time, the team arrived at a Pennsylvania dirt track after the track had experienced several days of rain. The rain had finally cleared and the sun had come out, but the sunshine did little to dry up the track. Huge puddles remained and posed a challenge to the performers, and as luck would have it, one large pool was directly in front of the takeoff ramp. The Doug Danger jump was the highlight of the show, so it would not be complete without the featured ramp-to-ramp jump.

"The track crew worked all day," Doug explained. But despite all their attempts to drain it or fill it in, they couldn't get rid of that enormous puddle that measured approximately 20-feet long and at least 8 inches deep. Still, as stated before, the show must go on.

As Doug recalls, "I went to Tim [Chitwood] and told him I'd take some speed runs through the puddle and watch the speedometer to see how much I slowed down going through it. Then I'd add that speed to the roll up to the ramp to achieve the ideal speed I needed for the jump."

"What was Tim's response?" I asked.

Smiling, Doug responded, "With a grin and a shrug of his shoulders, Tim said, 'Well, it looks good on paper,' and walked away, shaking his head."

"Did you do it?" I asked.

"I nailed it!" Doug responded with a laugh.

But a day later, he got a call that shook him to the bone. Todd Seeley, his longtime friend and confidante, had been killed in a horrific crash while performing a jump on a Honda TRX 250R quad (4-wheel ATV).

"With Todd's death, it really sunk in that what I'm doing here is serious! I was convinced I could do anything. I began to believe the myth that I was invincible. Heck, I even came back from the crash that put me in a coma! But Todd was not coming back! Everyone thinks you're brave. You don't think that way; you just think you know what you are doing. But I learned the real danger that day. Todd was a great performer—a perfectionist—yet he made a series of minor mistakes that cost him his life. At 95-100 mph, you aren't talking about sustaining injuries; you're talking about certain death, plain and simple. The body can only take so much. It was a shock and an eye-opener to me. With that, I realized I'd better smarten up!"

Doug went on to describe a second awakening after the death of his good friend and mentor, Evel Knievel. "Looking at Evel in that coffin made me realize that we are all human beings with frailties." Holding back tears, Doug continued, "Heck, Evel was a legend and in my eyes, invincible. I realized then that death is inevitable; it's always closer than we realize.

"So, I've lived my life to the fullest, with no regrets. I'm always careful to acknowledge those who have helped me along the way and let my family and friends know they are appreciated," he stated in a somber tone. "But it was Todd's [Seeley] death that was a hard lesson: pay attention to even the smallest details. It'll kill you if you don't," Doug strained to manufacture the merest hint of a smile as he concluded his thoughts.

"I learned so much from them: Evel, Tim [Chitwood], and Todd. I was so appreciative of their knowledge, skills, showmanship, and most importantly, their friendship. They all went too soon."

I'm sure Tim Chitwood, who passed in 2015, would reciprocate those thoughts. It was evident to me, having spent time with Tim, that he was also very appreciative of his friendship and partnership with Doug.

Keeping it in Check

Doug's demeanor is a good lesson for all of us, and he's different from other celebrities and success stories, in that, through it all, he has remained able to keep himself in check and to recognize when he was getting caught up in his own myth. This is a form of emotional intelligence that is sadly lacking in many people, but it is something we all should be striving for: humility, self-assessment, and attention to detail.

Then and today, Doug will tell you that his successes would not be possible without serious commitment to his craft and the support of those around him—his friends and family. Spend just a little time with Doug before an event or when he's with family and friends, and it becomes blatantly obvious that he's dead serious about both. Kindness towards others is always his first priority.

Chapter 9
Death is No Match for Me

"There is no more courageous person than one who looks death straight in the eye and doesn't blink."
~ Doug Danger ~

Photo courtesy of Marilyn Stemp

One Friday night in the spring of 2011, I received the call from Doug's mother.

"Have you talked to Doug lately?" she asked, obviously worried.

"No, I haven't seen him for a while. Why?" I inquired, suddenly fearing her response.

"He's in bad shape. I need you to check on him and be there if he needs you," my aunt replied in her sometimes-commanding voice. "He's got cancer, and it's really bad. He's gonna need some help—your help—and don't take no for an answer!"

I immediately called him. We discussed some of his predicament and agreed to meet for lunch at a local steakhouse…his suggestion.

When we arrived, my wife and I were warmly greeted by Doug and an absolutely stunning woman with long, flowing brunette hair, a nearly perfect figure, and a warm and inviting smile. She was up from Long Island, New York, helping Doug, and was the sister of Doug's close friend and fellow stuntman, Lou "Rocket" Re.

To our surprise, on the surface Doug appeared to be in reasonably good health, which was not how his mother had described him on the phone the day before.

We chatted a bit, got acquainted with his new friend Maria, and started to get caught up on what we each had missed during the extended time we hadn't seen each other.

Much like a decade before, just when it seemed like he'd finally "got his big break" and had embarked on an extremely well-paid, two-month tour of Australia, Doug had metaphorically hit a wall again. And this "wall" was just as dangerous and deadly as the wall he'd hit in that devastating, head-on crash a decade earlier.

He began to explain his predicament. "Right away, I started getting extremely tired and sleeping a lot while in Australia. I thought I was getting lazy. I tried to fight it by getting up earlier, but found I needed to take naps. I didn't know what was wrong. Then, not long into the tour, one of the guys in the show said, 'You look terrible. You need to visit a doctor and see what's going on.'"

Also around this time, Doug noticed a lump growing rapidly in his neck. "I thought maybe I got bitten by a spider or something."

So he went to the nearest hospital and ended up spending eight days there. During that time, they removed the lump and found that it was a tumor, not the bug bite he had suspected earlier. The Australian physicians informed him that they didn't know what had caused the tumor but that it was non-cancerous. 'Let it heal, and it should be okay,' was their instruction. Satisfied, and feeling much better, Doug rejoined the group to finish the tour.

Upon his return to the United States, Doug wasted no time scheduling an appointment with his doctor, who, after examining Doug, referred him to a specialist. He went for an evaluation with Dr. Wexler, who advised him that, 'If that lump comes back, get right back in here,' expressing that it sounded suspicious to him. After careful self-monitoring of the area, Doug noted that one month later the lump reappeared.

On a frigid Thursday afternoon, Doug called Maria and told her that he'd made arrangements to see Dr. Wexler the following Monday. At the appointment, the doctor scheduled a one-hour surgery. Doug and Maria arrived at the hospital, where Doug was prepped and taken off for the procedure. As Maria recalled, the anticipated one-hour procedure turned into an anxiety-filled, four-hour wait.

After the recovery period, Dr. Wexler approached Doug and Maria and delivered the news: a massive tumor was wrapped around Doug's tonsils and jugular vein. Though he didn't have the biopsy results to determine if the tumor was cancerous, the surgeon suspected that it was indeed malignant. Dr. Wexler went on to explain that he thought he had removed the entire tumor, but if the biopsy results reveal cancer, Doug would need radiation treatments to kill anything that remained. However, as a precautionary measure, Dr. Wexler scheduled an appointment with an oncologist, Dr. Siddiqui.

Doug arrived at the meeting with Dr. Siddiqui and was soon ushered into the doctor's office. Dr. Siddiqui somberly asked Doug to sit down as he settled himself behind his own desk and avoided direct eye contact with Doug. Doug recalled that it felt like one of those serious movie scenes where the doctor is about to deliver a terrible diagnosis.

"Don't say that. That usually means bad news," Doug laughed, referring to being asked to sit. He noted that Dr. Siddiqui didn't share in his amusement but remained serious and sober. He then slowly raised his head to look Doug straight in the eye.

"You have stage four cancer," Dr. Siddiqui stated in a firm, matter-of-fact voice. "At best, you likely have three to six months to live; you will need to get your affairs in order."

Doug sat motionless, his mouth agape but making no sound. Had he heard that right?

"Do you have a will?" Dr. Siddiqui continued.

Doug knew then that he had indeed heard the doctor correctly and quietly replied, "No."

The oncologist went on to say, "Well, start with that, and think about becoming an organ donor, if you're not one already."

Shocked, Doug remained silent and motionless. However, after a few more moments, he looked up at Dr. Siddiqui and questioned, "Hold on. You're telling me I have zero percent chance of beating this? By June, I'll be in the ground?"

The doctor continued in his professional doctor's voice, "With a stage four cancer diagnosis, the survival rate at this advanced stage is minimal at best. We've only seen a five percent survival rate, and that's if the treatment doesn't kill the patient first. You should have been treated immediately after your surgery in Australia." That had been four months ago.

Doug's ears perked up when he heard "five percent survival rate," and he smiled. "There's a five percent chance? That means five people out of a hundred beat this! So, I do have a chance! Do you know who I am? I'm Doug Danger, and far less than five percent of the people in the world do what I do for a living. Trust me. I will be one of those five percent. You do what you need to do to save my life, and tell me exactly what I have to do."

"It was still one of the toughest days of my life," Doug recalled. "Maria and I went to St. Patrick's church in Monson, Massachusetts. They have a statue of St. Peregrine, the Patron Saint of cancer patients and the sick. Together, we prayed that I'd live through this battle so I could be there for my kids."

He'd prayed, "God, my kids need me. Please let me be there for them until they grow up and are set in life. If you can get me beyond that, you can take me. Can you work that deal with me?"

Doug went on to say that, after praying, he began to cry. He and Maria sat there in that church, arm-in-arm, just the two of them, for over an hour. Doug wiped away his tears and at that time put his trust in the power of God. He felt ready to face the oncologist the next day for the treatment plan.

"For me, the power of prayer worked. I had to focus on going forward. I had many things to do while I was still on this Earth, and I was ready to put my plan into action," Doug stated.

"My follow-up appointment with Dr. Siddiqui was the next day," Doug noted. For the first time in a long time, he was more appreciative of the day being sunny and warm for a winter's day, stating that it was just the type of day where positive thoughts feel natural and goals all seem achievable.

"That's when I told him, right off, that I had no intention of dying from this cancer," Doug said firmly. "So Dr. Siddiqui said, 'There's a new experimental chemotherapy treatment available, but it's going to knock the living shit out of you, and in the end it could kill you. Do you want to try?"

"I said, 'Let's do it!'" Doug recalled with a shake of his fist.

"Funny, the doctor said, he knew I'd want to fight this diagnosis and he had already scheduled the first treatment for the next morning," Doug informed me with a wide-eyed grin.

To this day, Dr. Siddiqui will tell you that when Doug said those words the doctor knew he was on the path to a successful outcome, because defeating cancer starts with a winning attitude!

Just as Doug concluded this portion of the story, we were interrupted by the young waitress. "Excuse me, are you ready to order?"

The ladies ordered from the lunch menu first, and then I ordered. To my surprise, Doug pointed to the dinner menu and said, "I will have this steak dinner. Well, actually, make that two steak dinners."

He must have picked up on my puzzled look, because he turned to me and said, "Hey, I was given an order to pack on the weight while I'm in treatment. I've got contracts for shows in June. I don't go back on my word. I need to keep my strength up. I also told the doctor we need to pick up the pace with these chemotherapy treatments 'cuz I gotta be ready for these shows."

Oh yeah, he ate both meals, and if my memory serves me right, he even ordered dessert! Incredibly, he was able to pack on a good 45 pounds. And even with side effects of chemotherapy and radiation, his weight never got below 160 pounds.

Throughout his cancer treatments, Doug's physicians continued to voice concerns over his anticipated return to jumping in June. Maria remembers telling one physician that his plan to do the June shows was what was keeping Doug positive and moving forward. If the June shows were to be canceled, they might as well stop treatment and let him die now, because, not having a goal would surely do him in anyway.

Did Doug make the June shows? Absolutely!

Was the recovery tough? Yes, incredibly tough! There were numerous days when Doug literally had to crawl around his home to get anywhere.

Moreover, by the time the show schedule began, he was unquestionably not ready to resume performing, because during his second show he was in such a weakened state that he was unable to hang onto the motorcycle upon landing, resulting in a crash.

"I broke a finger and separated my shoulder," Doug later explained. "I did two shows that first day. I was dead tired from the heat and already worn out from the show earlier that day. Fortunately, I had time to recuperate before the third show."

Doug is a man of his word. Despite his weakened state, he'd promised to perform and was not going to let anything get in the way of him keeping those promises! He never missed one show, even though he was still receiving radiation therapy treatments, was in a state of overall weakness, and had to recover from injuries sustained on his second day back on the road.

I also have to confess that I never did help Doug at home as his mother requested, because for the entire six months, he had the help of that stunning lady we had met at lunch: Maria. She was there throughout his cancer treatments and performances; in fact, she never left his side. She married him in 2013, breaking her little brother's heart. Rocket Re jokingly says that the only regret he has in his entire stunt career is introducing his older sister to Doug Danger!

Doug underwent three rounds of chemotherapy for five days each round, and he received radiation treatment every day for seven weeks. Incredibly, he defied the odds when his cancer went into remission. Then, through grit, determination, and sheer willpower, he amazed the healthcare professionals by defeating cancer altogether. In 2012, Doug was told he was cancer free, and he has remained that way to this day!

Chapter 10
A Tale of Two Legends

"If you have a dream and the willpower to pursue it, any human being can be whoever he wants to be – it takes real determination."
~ **Doug Danger** ~

In 2013, at Evel Knievel Days in Butte, Montana, Lou Re introduced Doug Danger to Lathan McKay. McKay is an actor, American historian, producer, screenwriter, entrepreneur, professional skateboarder, and the largest Evel Knievel collector in the world. He went on to co-create the Evel Knievel Museum in Topeka, Kansas, which opened in June of 2017.

"Lathan is a passionate Evel Knievel collector. At the time I met him, he had already accumulated an impressive amount of rare and valuable Evel Knievel memorabilia and other personal items. It was so cool," recalled Doug. "Turns out, he was also a Doug Danger fan; we instantly became good friends."

"Hey, you're not going to believe what I just bought," McKay teased Doug. "I have it on display down on Main Street." Finally, he revealed he purchased a 1972 Harley-Davidson XR750, once owned and jumped by Evel Knievel himself. Doug went nuts. "Let's go! Come on, I have to see this," he exclaimed.

As Doug arrived on Main Street and walked into the display, he said, "My hair stood up on the back of my neck, and I got chills all over. It was like stepping back into my childhood. I stood in awe, just looking at it. It had the original 'Evel' in gold leaf painted on the tank and red, white, and blue stripes all around the outside. Then Lathan freaked me out! He said, 'Go ahead; sit on it.'"

"Are you kidding me? I'm going to sit on the King's bike?" Doug was hesitant as he approached the iconic motorcycle, threw his leg over the seat, and slowly sat down.

"I instantly went into another world," Doug explained. He raised his hands and reenacted the experience of sitting on that bike, demonstrating grabbing the bars and moving his body to get comfortable on the imaginary seat.

"It was similar to a spiritual moment—like Evel's spirit had entered my body, and I became Evel for a minute. I don't know how long I sat there, but it could have been a half-hour. I imagined the takeoff ramp coming towards me as I pretended to ready myself for the jump. People were all around and talking to me, but I couldn't hear what they were saying. It was like I was in a trance."

Lathan then stated to Doug, "How's it fit?" Doug turned his head, looked straight into Lathan's eyes, and said, "The word fear does not exist in my vocabulary," a famous quote from Evel. The whole room broke into laughter.

Eventually, bringing himself back to Earth and getting up off the bike, he turned his attention back to his new friend, Lathan McKay.

"Right there, right then, I told him that if he ever wanted this bike jumped again, I was the guy to do it. If not me, then it should be Robbie [Knievel]. No one else," he continued. "Lathan looked at me, smiled, and said, 'There's no way this bike will ever fly again. I just paid $350,000 for it. It's going straight to the museum.'"

However, several months later, Doug received a call from McKay. "You still want to jump that bike?" McKay asked. "I've got someone in Texas who is willing to pay a lot of money to see it fly again. What do you think?"

"The promotor for the jump wanted me to jump four or five cars at what is called the ROT [Republic of Texas] Rally in Austin, Texas. There's no way I was going to jump only five cars. Right there, on the phone, without even thinking it over, I said it had to be 15 cars. If I'm going to jump Evel's bike, it has to be big. So we settled on 15, and a date was set," Doug finished with a smile and a nod of his head.

Doug arrived two weeks ahead of time to build the ramps. Ken Galyas, a storied craftsman who was already known for building Robbie Knievel's ramps, erected an incredibly precise setup. He had to fine-tune the ramps and adjust the angles to handle flying the 350-pound machine with virtually no suspension. Doug performed just a few practice jumps to grow accustomed to the bike. Then they stretched out the ramps and put the fifteen cars in place for the leap the following day.

Doug Danger with Kenny Galyas

Doug then returned to his hotel to mentally prepare for the upcoming jump. The historic jump was nearly canceled, however, when a small tornado touched down on the ROT Rally grounds that night.

After the storm, and on that same evening, Doug received a call at the hotel telling him the bad news. His ramps had been knocked over by the high winds. He and the crew immediately rushed to the Rally to inspect the damage. When they arrived, they discovered that the specially constructed takeoff ramp had been flipped on its side and was now splintered beyond repair.

"It was all doom and gloom," he described. "Everyone thought we should cancel. My first response was, 'The jump is tomorrow; we have plenty of time to build another ramp. Let's get going.' So we did. You just gotta stay calm, believe in yourself, and make things happen!"

Amazingly, Ken Galyas and the team went to work and put the final nail in the ramp 20 minutes before the show was scheduled to start.

On June 14, 2014, in front of over 10,000 bikers and Texas locals, Doug magically and majestically flew Evel Knievel's 1972 Harley-Davidson XR750—a bike unchanged since Evel last used it—over 15 cars lined side-by-side and into the annuls of motorcycle history.

To the observer, it looked like the jump ended with a smooth-as-butter landing, but Doug later said that it definitely had not.

Republic of Texas Rally, Austin, Texas 2014
Photo courtesy of Michael Lichter © 2015

"I flew way too far and landed near the bottom of the ramp. It hit hard, but the landing was perfect. It could have been a lot worse had I not twisted the throttle wide-open just before touching down. Hey, I was happy that old bike didn't break in half," he laughed.

You would think the story would end there, with the storied $350,000 museum piece safely put away and preserved for generations of Evel Knievel fans at the soon-to-be-built Evel Knievel Museum. But no. With that leap, McKay was hooked and presumably convinced that Doug Danger could "safely" accomplish more jumps on Evel's motorcycle. Now he had a vision of recreating those long-ago Evel Knievel nostalgic moments with Doug Danger, and only Doug Danger. He trusted no one else at this point.

With Doug's blessing, Lathan quickly brokered a deal at one of the most spectacular venues for motorcycle enthusiasts for a once-in-a-lifetime world record motorcycle jump. The place? The legendary Sturgis Buffalo Chip Campground in Sturgis, South Dakota. There, Doug would jump the bike again for the upcoming 75th Anniversary of the Sturgis Bike Rally. Officials expected it to be the largest attended bike rally in world history, and it was. Doug decided he would leap over 22 cars on the same historic motorcycle in front of tens of thousands of fans attending the Buffalo Chip and hundreds of thousands viewing live on an internet simulcast.

Why 22 cars? Because no one had ever jumped an old (or new) Harley-Davidson over that many cars. Evel Knievel had tried, but only cleared 21 cars. He hung on, but the record stayed at 21. More recently, another jumper nearly lost his life attempting to beat the record by jumping 22 cars on a modern Harley-Davidson XR750 (with modern suspension). Doing this leap on a 43 year-old motorcycle was suicidal, some said. Hence, it was dubbed by Rod "Woody" Woodruff, the owner of the Buffalo Chip, as "The Suicide Jump."

Cheating Death in the Dakotas

Not wanting to miss history in the making, my wife and I packed up our Victory motorcycle and set out on a cross-country trip to Sturgis for our first-ever visit to the famed biker destination.

Several problems were plaguing a successful leap from the start. First, from the jump in Austin, Doug learned that the engine on Evel's XR750 was not a racing motor, but a mere stock replacement from 1972 that Evel Knievel had reportedly installed. Doug calculated that it would require a speed of exactly 80 miles per hour to leap it over the 22 cars successfully, but in its current form, the bike was only capable of reaching roughly 76 miles per hour.

"We didn't want to retrofit it with oversized pistons and modify the motor. This bike was historic. It had to remain preserved and stock," Doug emphasized. "We couldn't change the gearing either, as it already had the largest front sprocket that would fit, and the smallest possible rear sprocket. I know now why Evel had all those problems with gearing back then."

Having this obvious gearing issue, Doug enlisted the help of two motorcycle mechanic friends who made the trek out to Sturgis with a massive trailer: Gene Payne and Dennis Tomczak - their trailer resembled a rolling garage; it held everything imaginable to work on a motorcycle. This Michigan-based team with over 75-years of combined experience had wrenched on XR750s for the dirt-track famed "Michigan Mafia," whose riders were winners of numerous motorcycle flat-track championships. Doug hoped that these specialists could also work some magic on the jump bike and get it prepared for what once seemed an impossible task. Their goal was to tune the XR750 so it was able to obtain, at the very least, the 80 miles per hour needed to gap the 122 feet between the ramps.

L to R, Gene Payne, Dennis Tomczak, Doug Danger, Robbie Hull, and Lathan McKay

Fortunately, there was a slight downhill on the approach before the land flattened out at the jump site, because despite their skillful tuning of the carburetors and advancing of the timing, the mechanics were unable to give Doug any more than 78 miles per hour on flat ground. All that could be hoped for was that the slight downhill on the approach to the ramps was enough to propel the motorcycle two miles per hour faster. Compounding the problem, one of the mechanics worriedly told me, "Never mind the tuning. Good God, man, the bike is 43 years old. These parts could fail at any time. I just hope it stays running." This news was not comforting, to say the least.

Despite what looked to the bystander to be a "smooth-as-butter" landing that year in Austin, Texas, practice jump landings earlier in the week were brutal at 30, then 20 feet shorter than the forthcoming record jump. The three inches of front suspension was violently bottoming out almost immediately upon landing, and the back shocks were severely "pogo-ing," a motocross slang term referring to the rear shocks rapidly rebounding back out after being compressed. This abrupt reaction can toss an unexpected rider clean over the handlebars, very similar to how an angry bull throws a rodeo cowboy over or onto the bull's head. It ain't pretty.

Going into the days leading up to the jump, Doug began to wonder if he'd bitten off more than he could chew. He was worried. McKay was also concerned, and so were Doug's wife and crew. Despite all their efforts to conceal it, everyone's anxiety was evident.

"Doug, I'm troubled by the bike's suspension. Can we adjust it?" one friend asked.

"Yeah, it's really rough on landings," Doug responded. "Show me what you are thinking."

Doug then grabbed his phone and pulled up the video of the last practice jumps, as a number of the crew gathered around to view the landings.

"Right there, see? (He pointed to the landing.) It almost kicked you over the bars. I'm afraid you won't be able to hang on if we don't do something about that," the crew member said, profoundly concerned. The others chimed in with agreement.

On the rear of the bike was an old set of flat-track shocks once used by Mike Patterson, owner of Historic Harley-Davidson, when he raced back in the day. They were more modern than 1972 shocks, but just barely, and definitely not designed for jumping.

"How do we slow the rebound on these? Does anyone know how to adjust these shocks?" Doug asked.

Well over 220 years of motorcycle racing and wrenching experience were sitting at that campsite that evening. They needed to make a decision on suspension adjustments, but there would be no opportunity to test that decision, since another practice jump was not possible now that the fans had rolled into the Buffalo Chip.

After some online research and phone calls to racer friends, someone miraculously found and sent a photo of the shock's repair manual to the team. From there, a long and grueling debate was held among some of the most opinionated (but knowledgeable) men I've ever had the pleasure of meeting, resulting in the suspension being "dialed in" for that fateful day. It had to be, to avoid inevitable disaster.

You see, if the crew had not corrected the suspension, I am convinced that the beautiful, legendary motorcycle would have crashed and been destroyed beyond repair, and that Doug Danger, well beyond his 53rd birthday, might have made his last leap on this Earth. For Doug, it had to be an educated and absolutely perfect suspension adjustment—a life-saving decision for a 43 year-old bike flying a "well-seasoned" 53 year-old man a distance that had never been flown before.

Making things worse, some former stuntmen and naysayers were making predictions that this would be the day Doug Danger died. One motorcycle jumper going as far as to text Doug numerous times to tell him of his prediction, only adding to the pressures leading up to the world record attempt.

Doug was unusually solemn and noticeably worried for several days leading up to the jump, a demeanor alien to him, and one I'd never seen before. It only increased my fear.

August 6th, 2015, was a beautiful, sunny day, not always typical for that time of year in that part of South Dakota. A slight breeze was coming in the direction of travel (going toward the takeoff ramp at Doug Danger's back), so it would not be a hindrance. The temperature was just right, warm but not overly warm. Concerned about the approach to the ramp and the speed needed to leap this incredible distance, the crew from the Buffalo Chip had laid down 900 feet of sand on the path to the approach to the takeoff ramp and layered thick rubber stadium flooring over it; the sight was a welcome relief.

Starting early, the crew skillfully lined up 22 cars (owned by the campers at the Buffalo Chip) side-by-side. They carefully aligned the takeoff and landing ramps in place at each end of the cars.

On the landing ramp side, the venue placed hundreds of hay bales to protect vendors and their wares from a possible out-of-control 1972 Harley-Davidson XR750 motorcycle. Far too close to the bottom of the landing ramp sat a large building. It was just yards away and barely to the right of safe travel. The crew also lined hay bales up against it, but the straw seemed to comfort no one.

The television crew readied cameras and cables, being sure to bury the wires so as not to cause havoc and allow for smooth speed-runs past the takeoff ramp on a bike not designed to absorb bumps and surely not designed to fly.

Cement barriers and roped-off areas kept the spectators from interfering with the jump and helped protect them in the event of a crash.

The asphalt landing area was swept clean of dirt and debris, allowing for a clean surface to ensure a safe stopping distance before the hay bales and the wall of vendors.

Just before the festivities began, Doug had a last-minute gathering with his crew and then some quiet time with his wife Maria, to say a prayer and bolster his strength.

As the time of the event drew near, the enthusiastic crowd packed into the arena. Every person squeezing into the spectator areas was a motorcycle and Doug Danger fan. They were all excited to not only see Doug accomplish this feat, but to remember and pay tribute to the legend, Evel Knievel.

The tribute also included some help from Vanson Leathers, of Fall River, Massachusetts, who made an exact replica of one of Evel's leathers for this jump—cape and all. Additionally, Robbie Hull, an artist and friend of Doug's, hand-painted a replica of Evel's helmet for him. On the day of the show, Lathan McKay surprised Doug, handing him Evel Knievel's actual diamond-studded cane to carry. All of these touches were perfect complements to what was to be a spectacular day. It was all up to Doug now, just the way he liked it.

Estimates from the Buffalo Chip put the crowd somewhere between 35,000 to 45,000 excited fans. The venue provided an array of entertainment for onlookers as they situated themselves. Videos of Doug Danger were playing on the two "jumbotrons." A female Doug Danger fan, sporting only painted-on Doug Danger stars and stripes, paraded around, keeping many entertained. That particular surprise was arranged by the Buffalo Chip for all the adoring fans!

"Sturgis! Are you ready? Sturgis! Are you ready?" the announcer, Doug Klang, excitedly screamed out.

"Let me ask you to turn your attention to the video screens." Klang directed the crowd to the two video monitors. The crowd grew silent and watched a masterfully directed Doug Danger introduction. On the video, they saw Doug and Maria as a kind and loving couple explaining why this couldn't be a suicide jump. They asserted that Doug had far too much left to do as a husband, father, and friend. It was a message of hope and inspiration, coupled with Doug Danger's trademark directive to "follow your dreams."

Just as the video ended, spectators heard the roar of a motorcycle off in the distance—the beautiful and distinct sound of a Harley-Davidson V-twin. The sound grew noticeably louder as Doug Danger entered the arena, wearing his signature leathers and cape, both of which were a tribute that day to the original owner of this motorcycle, Evel Knievel. He rode to the bottom of the landing ramp, killed the motor, handed the bike to a waiting crew member, and walked to the top of the landing ramp to address the masses. The announcer bellowed out to the crowd, "Ladies and gentlemen, it is my pleasure to introduce to you the man considered to be the greatest motorcycle jumper of all time, Doug Danger!"

Doug grasped the microphone and proceeded to tell the story about his miraculous defeat of cancer, as he had so many times before. He said he intended to take that same spirit with him as he conquered the seemingly impossible challenge before him. The throngs of bikers intently hung on his every word. When he concluded, the crowd erupted and continued to applaud as he remounted the motorcycle and prepared his mind for the task at hand.

With a push from Lathan and another crew member, the XR750 came back to life. Doug gave one more wave to the 35,000-plus onlookers and headed back to the starting point to begin a series of speed runs.

"At that point, I still had no idea whether I was going to be able to get to the 80 miles per hour I needed," Doug recalled about that day. "I made that first speed run and got to 80, but as I hit the crossroad about 200 feet before the takeoff ramp, I took some air off a bump in the road, and when I landed, I looked down at the speedometer to see I was only going 78 as I approached the takeoff area. That wasn't going to be fast enough. My heart sank; I thought I was a dead man."

Doug flew by the takeoff ramp and then the landing ramp at blazing speed for such a tight area. He turned around and nodded lovingly at his worried wife, who paced near the landing area. He tried not to let her see his deep concern.

He returned to the beginning of the 900-foot run to the jump site and rode up to one of the Buffalo Chip security personnel.

"I need more speed," he yelled to the security guard. "I need these people cleared out of the way up to that water tower," Doug pointed to a water tower about 500 feet away.

Immediately, the security guard took charge, and in less than a minute, he and some other crew members working with him herded the people safely out of the way.

"Now, I had a much needed 1400-foot run," Doug recalled.

With his heart pounding, he gassed it. Holding it wide open, he shifted through the gears, hitting that crossroad and small jump at 81 miles per hour. Upon landing, he was going 79 miles per hour.

"I said a prayer and kept the throttle pinned to the stop as I flew by the takeoff ramp," Doug reminisced.

He turned around and rode in the opposite direction, slower than usual, before making another U-turn and driving up the takeoff ramp to give his trademark thumbs-up to the crowd. This ride to the top of the takeoff ramp was the indication that, unless he needed to call off the run at the last minute, this next run to the ramps would be for the record attempt.

Doug recalled, "I made my way back to the starting point, thinking I was going to die. After all, I was 53 year-old man. If I crashed, I was not going to survive it. I knew that."

Doug turned the bike around at the starting point and said his prayer.

"I reached out to God and said, 'I hope you're ready for me, Lord, because here I come.' I honestly thought I was a dead man. But, I did what I said I would. I let that clutch out and was off."

"Funny, once you begin your run, the fear goes away," Doug explained. "It's simply business and instinct."

I hit the bump at the crossroad at 81 miles per hour and took air, but never let off [of the throttle]. I was sure I had lost a few miles per hour but kept it pinned," he described.

As he neared the takeoff ramp, he glanced down and registered that he was going 79 miles per hour again, but he continued to hold that throttle wide open as he launched into the air.

"There's no fear up there. I've been doing this for over forty years now. It's business—just instinct and experience. In flight, you make the necessary adjustments and prepare for the landing."

Buffalo Chip Campground, Sturgis, South Dakota 2015
Photo courtesy of Chad Coppess

To the naked eye, the flight looked masterful and perfectly level. However, likely because of the full-throttle takeoff, the back wheel began to drift to the right—a dreaded cross-up! Oh no, could this be his kiss of death?

Doug said, "To my surprise, as I flew through the air, I realized I did have enough speed to clear the distance. I saw the safety ramp, then the top of the landing ramp pass by as I rolled the throttle to wide open again just before touchdown."

Hanging on, and into history

To me, from my angle standing near the takeoff ramp, it seemed inevitable that the crossed-up landing was going to end in a crash. I was not in the best position to view the landing, so as he touched down, I couldn't see what was happening. A picture-perfect landing, in light of the circumstances, looked hopeless to me.

So, you can imagine my confusion when I saw the crew instantly raise their arms in celebration. How could he have held on? Then, to my surprise and delight, he came back into my view, miraculously still on that bike. I was able to breathe a sigh of relief.

The landing was brutal. Video replay revealed that the impact ripped Doug Danger's hand from the handlebars as he hit the plywood with a loud thud. He experienced a scary "death wobble" as he fought to correct the cross-up and bring the celebrated Harley-Davidson to a stop.

Unbelievably, Doug Danger was able to wrangle the motorcycle into alignment and into the history books.

With a fist pump, he celebrated his accomplishment, then swung the motorcycle around and triumphantly rode to the top of the landing ramp. From the deafening cheers of the fans, it was apparent that they were well aware they had just witnessed a once-in-a-lifetime, history-making event.

Doug hugged his wife and most of his crew, then turned, grabbed the microphone and yelled out to the cheering fans, "This is not about beating my friend, Evel Knievel. This was just me finishing the jump for him. Now Evel and I hold this record together."

A relieved Mrs. Danger, Maria Senecal, greets her husband.

Doug Danger celebrates the historic accomplishment with the cheering Sturgis crowd.

Notwithstanding his world record of 42 cars, Doug later described the Buffalo Chip jump as the most fulfilling and challenging jump of his life. I know I witnessed the impossible that day.

With the same bike and with a very trusting friend, Lathan McKay, at his side, Doug made a return to Texas's ROT Rally to leap over a fire truck. And, in Topeka, Kansas he jumped over the entire fleet of that city's police vehicles for the 2017 grand opening of the Evel Knievel Museum with ten pounds of video cameras attached to his helmet. Finally returning to the Buffalo Chip later that year to, yet again, leap the Harley-Davidson XR750 motorcycle 141 feet over a tank of rattlesnakes.

Buffalo Chip Campground, Sturgis, South Dakota 2017

Do you want to experience what it's like to jump over 15 police cars on Evel Knievel's very own motorcycle? Well, you can! The Evel Knievel Museum in downtown Topeka, Kansas, adjacent to Historic Harley Davidson, features a virtual reality jump where you can experience the feat just like Doug Danger!

Downtown Topeka, Kansas 2017

Downtown Topeka, Kansas 2017

Chapter 11
Riding Into the Sunset

"Dreams are great. Having the courage to pursue your dreams is what will make them happen. Don't ever lose sight."
~ **Doug Danger** ~

Recently, Doug Danger talked to me about addressing a group of junior high school kids. He told me that at these school assemblies he usually gives an anti-drug, anti-bullying, or motivational speech that includes

~ 183 ~

never losing sight of your big dreams. One part of these assemblies always consists of a recap of his jumping career, including his mishaps. He made note that he may need to rethink the part where he "brags" about all of his broken bones.

During one of these assemblies, a kid raised his hand and asked, "How many broken bones have you had?"

"Fifty-nine," Doug proudly boasted.

"Boy, you must not be very good," the young man quickly replied.

"Damn, that kid had a good point," Doug said with a chuckle.

Notwithstanding this kid's observation, one cannot overlook the fact that Doug Danger has been performing stunts for over four decades and has completed many thousands of jumps. He's also a hero, not only because of his accomplishments, but because of the man he is. He always takes time to sign autographs and meet with fans—adults and kids alike. Humility is his strength and perhaps also his worst enemy. Unselfishly giving of his time is his nature. Some might say this generosity has devalued him monetarily over the years, but I don't think he would have had it any other way.

Making a big deal of himself isn't in his game. He still remembers being that enamored kid at Caesar's Palace, anxiously awaiting a glimpse of Evel Knievel, and never forgetting that feeling. I guess you can say he realizes that he still puts his leathers on one leg at a time.

Before it was a Thing

What you may not realize is that long before the days of extreme motorcycle jumping tricks (such as you see in the X-Games), Doug Danger was experimenting with tricks. For example, he innovated the no-hand leap by taking both hands off the handlebars in mid-flight. In the early '80s, this move was quite the show-stopper.

In late 2019, while preparing for a nationally televised stunt show, *Evel Live 2*, Doug got a chance to meet supercross and freestyle motocross pioneer Travis Pastrana and spend some time at the Pastrana compound.

Doug recalls: "We were touring the property in a 4-seater side-by-side, and off in the distance, I saw all his freestyle ramps. They vary in height and steepness and are positioned in a way that you can leap off one and catch the next one or vice-versa."

Spotting an unusually large, wide ramp, Doug asked, "What do you use that ramp over there for?"

"Do you really want to know?" smiled Pastrana.

"'Yeah,' I said, thinking he was going to tell me," Doug recounted. "Then Travis said, 'Hang on!' He flipped it around, hauled ass towards the ramp and…wham! We launched into the air with a sandpit about 50 feet higher than the takeoff and 70 to 80 feet away. At the highest point, we were above the trees. Before you knew it, we landed smoothly—not using up even half of the suspension. It was incredible."

"Because I know how to jump so well, I understood how skillful that feat was," Doug continued. "It isn't just foolish luck that got us to hit so smoothly and perfectly on the other side; it was the skill of a supercross champion with all the years of devoted practice to his craft. I understand the perfection it took to do that feat; I watched him. As we got up in the air, he gave a tap of the hand brake to bring the buggy's front end down slightly to ensure a safe and smooth flight. Then, just before the landing, he raced up the throttle just enough to bring the front end up, resulting in an absolutely smooth, nearly perfect landing," Doug demonstrated a perfect landing with his right hand.

It was then that Pastrana turned to Doug and exclaimed, "I can't believe I'm hanging out with

Doug Danger!" He went on to say that Doug Danger had inspired him when he was younger.

"Wow," said Doug. "And the whole time I'm thinking, 'I can't believe I'm hanging out with Travis Pastrana!'"

From one daredevil to another, he recognized that Pastrana was a master at his craft, having developed his skills over time, with a great deal of practice. He understood better than anyone the hours of relentless practice on the motocross and supercross tracks that it would take to perfect skills to that level.

Success in life takes hard work and dedication. Anyone you see who's a master at their craft was not a master at first. More than likely, they stunk at it when they first tried. Oh, some get lucky for a while. However, they will fail in the end without total dedication and a clear understanding that the threat of failure is always knocking at the door.

Some professionals may tell you they've been "lucky" to have done something for so long, but one earns "luck" through hard work, determination, and a no-quit attitude. When a pro is good they make it look easy, but I can honestly tell you it is not!

Stopping to Smell the Roses

Two readily apparent characteristics you will always notice when you look at Doug Danger are his love for life and his love of people. Take the time to recognize your friends and family, he would tell you, and learn to appreciate each day. Never stop chasing your dream, and don't forget to stop along the way and be thankful for what you have today.

In that spirit, and because of his love for motorcycles, Doug and his wife Maria moved from Massachusetts to settle in the much warmer state of Florida, near the Daytona area. Living there has allowed them to enjoy riding year-round, and spend time riding with Doug's mother, better known as "Mom Danger," who continues to ride even though she is now into her 80s.

L to R, Doug Danger, Marge "Mom Danger," and the author, Steve Hall

Equally as important, Doug prioritizes spending quality time with his wife, Maria—the love of his life.

"This lady puts up with a lot," he stated in a serious tone. "I know it ain't easy being married to me, so I show her how much I appreciate her love and friendship as often as I can."

Doug still performs stunts in front of tens of thousands of fans each year with his long-time friend Jack Brady, of KSR Motorsports. Although Doug won't turn down another big jump, he has also found other interests to keep him busy. He dabbles in real estate and travels to different venues for speaking engagements.

Chapter 12
Doubt, Fear, and Other Demons

"Once you commit to the task at hand, instinct and experience kick in, leaving no room for fear to come along for the ride."
~ Doug Danger ~

"**M**r. Senecal, you're never going to amount to anything!"

"Forget your foolish dreams; you aren't going to be successful unless you know the right people. You don't."

"With the extent of your injuries, you'll never jump again; you'll be lucky if you even walk again."

"You need to get your things in order because you can't beat this cancer; it's too late."

"If you go ahead with this jump, you're going to die."

These were only a few of the opinions that Doug Danger heard over the years from people he liked and respected! But obviously they were wrong—dead wrong. Where would he be now if he had believed just one of these negative statements? Fortunately, he was determined to prove the naysayers wrong.

Have you heard words of discouragement from people you like, love, or respect? Do they dishearten you, or make you doubt yourself? Do you have dreams, desires, and ideas that you keep locked inside? Many of us do.

Why do we hold back? Why do we put our dreams and desires on the back burner? We do it because of two mostly useless or overblown emotions: fear and doubt. Words of discouragement dance around and pop up at inopportune times, causing us to doubt ourselves. We also feel fear: the fear of failure, fear of non-acceptance, fear of ridicule, and/or fear of pain (emotional and physical).

As evidenced, Doug Danger had ample opportunity to give up on his dreams, and even more opportunities to quit in the face of adversity. Yet he didn't. Fear and doubt were simply another challenge to overcome and to defeat. He stayed focused on his goals, dreams, and desires and let nothing get in the way.

Doug will explain that there is a "sweet spot" when landing a nearly perfect jump. You want to come down near the top of the landing ramp, with the front wheel of the bike slightly higher than the rear, the RPM's of the motor going at the exact speed to help glide the bike forward, and the body ideally positioned in synch with the machine. All of these elements must be in harmony for a successful, smooth as butter landing to be executed.

Do Doug's jumps always go as planned? No. Sometimes Doug can't find the "sweet spot." So he learns from mistakes and moves on.

Focusing on where you want to be, while not dwelling on the past, is the key to success. Achievement of your goals, dreams, or desires is the "sweet spot" in your life.

Know that things will not always go as planned. Failing is a reality in all aspects of life. Failures are lessons. Learn from them, move on, and stay focused. Keep your attention on where you want to be, not on the distractions of doubt and fear. Remember *your* sweet spot.

Doug recalls the story of the great inventor, Thomas Edison. One story tells of how Edison tried nearly 1000 different materials for the filament of the lightbulb until he settled on one. Did he fail the first 999 times? No, said Edison. Each one was a confirmation of what didn't work, and brought him one step closer to knowing what material would work. Edison wasn't naturally gifted. Determination, hard work, and optimism were his tools. He focused on hitting his sweet spot and didn't allow anything else to distract him.

Doug is a perfect example of the truth that we are all far more capable of doing what we dream of or desire to do than we realize. The only things holding you back are discouragement, doubt, and fear. Breaking away from these three imaginary shackles is key to reaching your highest potential, including obtaining true happiness.

How do I know this? Because Doug Danger has been a rebel and a fighter since he was a young child. He refused to allow his circumstances to dictate his future. He dared to dream big, and despite adversity, he remained (and remains) optimistic.

Doug came from a broken family. He lived in poverty at an early age. He had to overcome seemingly insurmountable odds to recover from a devastating head injury, and he survived stage four cancer. Yet Doug Danger never lost hope. Despite hardship, he never lost sight of his goals and remains optimistic to this day. When he mastered a goal and fulfilled a dream, he simply added a new one to his bucket list and always looked toward the horizon for a new adventure and challenge.

A few years ago, Doug Danger jumped over a pit of the nastiest, angriest rattlesnakes you've ever seen. A fork truck held the rattlesnake pit up in the air, level with the top of the landing ramp. Doug made the jump on the same 1972 Harley Davidson XR750 at the Sturgis Buffalo Chip Campground in Sturgis, South Dakota, again. However, this time the gap between the ramps was 20 feet shorter than his world record jump two years earlier. It should have been a piece of cake for Doug Danger—well, not really, but hopefully. Yet, despite his decades of jumping knowledge and experience, he badly overshot the "sweet spot" and violently landed that antique bike at the very bottom of the landing ramp.

"Damn, Doug, what happened?" one crew member asked.

"Did you see those snakes?" Doug excitedly replied. "There was no way I was going to get anywhere near those things!" Doug Danger acknowledged later that his fear of rattlesnakes nearly resulted in a costly mistake. Keep those irrational fears in check.

A few years ago, shortly after a death in my family, I signed up to skydive with Doug and a couple of other friends. Almost immediately, I was scolded by other family members for being insensitive and perhaps even suicidal, but I went anyway.

On the afternoon of our skydiving adventure, I'll admit I was scared. But after some pre-jump training, I looked over at a grinning Doug then nervously turned to the instructor who soon would be strapped to my back.

"How many times have you jumped today?" I asked.

He smiled and said, "You are my eighth."

At that point, I realized my fear was irrational. To my skydiving instructor, this was just another day at the office.

One lesson Doug likes to pass onto others is that you are far more capable than you or others give you credit for. You are capable of doing and trying many, many things about which you dream. There is nothing that you can't do if you stop doubting yourself.

He won't claim that you'll be great at the task right from the start. But all the greats will tell you that greatness isn't something you are born with; it's taught, it's learned, and it's practiced.

Doug also emphasizes that his biggest fear is regret—another useless but powerful emotion.

First, dwelling on a past wrongdoing can destroy you. It drags you down. Learn from it, forgive yourself, and then move on.

Then there is the regret of not fulfilling an idea, goal, dream, or desire that you had burning inside you but you chose not to pursue for a variety of reasons. That regret hurts.

He goes on to say that he's met or heard of so many people who never pursued a dream, and almost every time, fear and/or doubt is what held them back.

He vowed at a very young age to not be that man who let fear and doubt get in his way. He vowed not to stash away his dreams, goals, and desires. You won't hear him say, "I should have tried that, but …." However, you may hear him say, "Wow, I won't do that again." There is a big difference between lessons learned and regrets!

We each have been given a gift of our one and only life. It is not fair to our creator, ourselves, our loved ones, or society in general if we don't achieve all we are capable of and all we desire. Moreover, if you don't seek the happiness you deserve, and you don't share your dreams and ideas with the world, are you truly *living* your life? Share your greatness and joy with the world! Live life to the fullest! No regrets!

Is there something you've dreamed of doing? If so, then make it happen.

Have something to say? Say it.

Are you looking to change careers? Apply for that job.

Want to go to college? Sign up today for your first class.

Want to write a book? Write a little today, then tomorrow.

Want to skydive or ride a motorcycle? Take a lesson.

Have the courage to uncover your potential. Have the courage to discover your sweet spot.

Chapter 13
Casting a Shadow

"For whatever reason, I believe God put me on this Earth to be Doug Danger. I don't take this responsibility lightly."
~ **Doug Danger** ~

In 2015, at the invitation of Doug and Maria, my wife and I made that trek out to Sturgis on our motorcycle to witness the historic jump and help if needed. What truly fascinated us was the dedication of other well-known stuntmen (his crew) who also made the trek at their own expense to help.

We already talked about the mechanics, Gene Payne, and Dennis Tomczak, who dropped everything, loaded up their trailer, and drove from Michigan. The incredible stuntman and announcer Doug Klang was also there from Southern California. Philip Thomas Guerrero, a motorcycle racer and collector (also from Southern California) came too. Lou "Rocket" Re, a stuntman, longtime friend, and Doug's brother-in-law made the trek from Long Island, New York. Bob Hendricks, a motorcycle mechanic and collector came out from Ohio. Dean Sasen, a musician and dedicated fan showed up from Massachusetts. Ken Galyas, a carpenter and long-time friend journeyed from Rhode Island. Robbie Hull, an artist from Austin, Texas made the trip, as did Lathan McKay, actor, producer, screenwriter and curator of the Evel Knievel Museum.

All of these people, talented and successful in their own right, dropped everything to be at an event assisting Doug, never asking for anything in return but to be part of motorcycle history.

When asked what brings them back, each one consistently talks about being part of a cohesive team and how Doug often reminds them of their importance and that his accomplishments would not be possible without them.

"He called me and said he needed me," one friend reiterated. "There's something about traveling 1,000 miles or more and being gone for two weeks to help accomplish something that's never been done before. It keeps drawing me back. There's something about it. I love it, and I love the guy."

Another stated, "It's being a part of something few others get to experience. It's being a part of history. But it's Doug who draws you there. You can't help but root for the guy."

Yet another stuntman said, "In this business, it's much less competitive than you'd think. We help each other out."

Stories like these have been commonplace throughout Doug Danger's career. Why? In my eye, Doug's leadership skills, combined with his good-hearted nature, plays a huge role in his success with people.

There are two types of leaders in this world: First, there is the short-tempered, angry, and insecure person who isn't in reality a leader at all. He or she manages and dictates using fear. This person is the opposite of a leader.

Then there is the visionary leader who, from the front, paints a picture of what the accomplishment of a goal, dream, or desire looks like. This leader doesn't demand respect; he or she earns respect and followers by demonstrating dignity and respect for others, especially their team. A consummate professional loves to teach and shares the credit, never basking in the glory without acknowledging those who made an accomplishment possible. This person casts a shadow much larger than himself and sees leadership as a calling with great responsibility that should never be abused.

As a leader and a visionary, Doug Danger has demonstrated those skills repeatedly. He is a man who, after accomplishing one of the greatest stunts of all time, gave credit to God and to his predecessor, Evel Knievel—humbly stating that he and Evel accomplished it together. He also shares the glory with his crew of misfits who believe in his vision and continue to follow him wherever he asks them to go.

Jumping over an L-1011 jumbo jet for the television show "I Dare You" in 2000

Today, when so much has changed and people long for days gone by, Doug Danger stands as a connection to this long-lost past. He is a man who says what he means and means what he says. When he gives his word, you can take that to the bank. He is a man who never lost sight of his humble beginnings and who makes time for his legion of fans, his friends, or a stranger in need. He is a man who, in the hope that he may save one person with his message, takes the time to seriously reflect on matters such as overcoming drugs, stamping out bullying, or defeating cancer. He is a man who truly wants you to never lose sight of your dreams. Doug Danger has the ability, even if only for a moment, to bring us back to a more innocent time.

In the decades that he has been performing motorcycle stunts - from his 149 foot long and 85 foot high leap off of a multi-story building into a hometown lake, a 160 foot jump over an L-1011 jumbo jet, 14 busses on a 125cc motorcycle, 18 tractor-trailer trucks, the world record overall long-distance jump of 42 cars, his leap over 22 cars aboard Evel's $350,000 museum piece, thousands of other stunts of wildly varying distances and hurdles, and lest we forget, overcoming a life-threatening head injury and defeated stage four cancer – Doug Danger has demonstrated incredible strength, courage, and perseverance throughout it all.

For the multitudes of fans that have been paying attention, Doug Danger has been the hero and escape that so many crave. Many fans have treasured their moment(s) with this humble star. Stories about how he changed someone's life with a word or an action are endless. Moreover, hundreds (maybe thousands) of people are privileged to utter the words, "My friend, Doug Danger." And to Doug, they *are* his friends. All of them.

Remember Doug's words, "You never know when your time is up. Be happy and smile. Live each day to the fullest with no regrets. Dare to dream."

About the Author

Steve Hall, who resides in Sturbridge, Massachusetts, is also the co-author of _15 Rules for a Loving, Lasting, and Satisfying Relationship_ with his wife, Janet. In addition, he is a healthcare executive, inventor, award-winning speaker, political candidate, and lifetime motorcycle rider, racer, and fan.

For Steve, it was an absolute honor and pleasure to help Doug Danger tell his phenomenal, inspirational story.

Thank you for taking the time to read it.

References

McCurdy, D. A. (2008). Find A Way. In D. A. McCurdy, Find A Way (p. 195). Adam Beck Publishing.

Museum, E. K. (2017). Evel Knievel Museum. 2047 SW Topeka Blvd, Topeka, Kansas, USA: Historic Harley-Davidson.

Roger Allers, R. M. (Director). (1994). The Lion King [Motion Picture].

Society, S. (1998, July 26). Obituary - Todd Seeley. Retrieved from Seeley Genealogical Society: http://www.seeley-society.net/obits-ey/obit-toddseeley.html

Made in the USA
Monee, IL
23 June 2020